Vagueness

REASON AND ARGUMENT

VOLUME 4

The titles published in this series are listed at the end of this volume.

Linda Claire Burns
University of Melbourne,
Australia

Vagueness

An Investigation into Natural Languages and the Sorites Paradox

KLUWER ACADEMIC PUBLISHERS
DORDRECHT / BOSTON / LONDON

Library of Congress Cataloging-in-Publication Data

Burns, Linda Claire, 1946-
Vagueness : an investigation into natural languages and the sorites paradox / Linda Claire Burns.
p. cm. -- (Reason and argument ; v. 4)
Includes bibliographical references and index.
ISBN 0-7923-1489-1 (acid-free paper)
1. Language and logic. 2. Ambiguity. 3. Sorites paradox. 4. Semantics (Philosophy) I. Title. II. Series.
P39.B87 1991
401'.43--dc20 91-36104

ISBN 0-7923-1489-1

Published by Kluwer Academic Publishers,
P.O. Box 17, 3300 AA Dordrecht, The Netherlands.

Kluwer Academic Publishers incorporates
the publishing programmes of
D. Reidel, Martinus Nijhoff, Dr W. Junk and MTP Press.

Sold and distributed in the U.S.A. and Canada
by Kluwer Academic Publishers,
101 Philip Drive, Norwell, MA 02061, U.S.A.

In all other countries, sold and distributed
by Kluwer Academic Publishers Group,
P.O. Box 322, 3300 AH Dordrecht, The Netherlands.

Printed on acid-free paper

Printed in the Netherlands

for Bea

Table of Contents

Part II–THE SORITES PARADOX

PREFACE

This work is in two parts. It began as a general investigation of vagueness in natural languages. The Sorites Paradox came to dominate the work however, and the second part of the book consists in an discussion of that puzzle and related problems. The first part contains a general discussion of the nature of vagueness and its sources. I discuss various conceptions of vagueness in chapter 1 and outline some of the problems to do with the conception of vagueness as a linguistic phenomenon. The most interesting of these is the Sorites paradox, which occurs where natural languages exhibit a particular variety of borderline case vagueness. I discuss some sources of vagueness of the borderline case variety, and views of the relation between linguistic behaviour and languages which are vague in this sense. I argue in chapter 2 that these problems are not to be easily avoided by statistical averaging techniques or attempts to provide a mathematical model of consensus in linguistic usage. I also consider in chapter 3 various approaches to the problem of providing an adequate logic and semantics for vague natural languages, and argue against two currently popular approaches to vagueness. These are supervaluation accounts which attempt to provide precise semantic models for vague languages based on the notion of specification spaces, and attempts to replace the laws of classical logic with systems of fuzzy logic.

I argue in the first part that borderline case vagueness is not the only variety of vagueness in natural language, and that vagueness is not only a linguistic phenomenon. Some of these arguments are taken up and the connexion between different varieties of vagueness investigated in the second half of the book.

The second part consists of a detailed examination of the Sorites paradox and the development of a novel solution to it. In chapter 4 I concentrate on an argument expounded by Michael Dummett and Crispin Wright which seems to show that languages vague in the strong borderline case sense defined in chapter 1 are incoherent. Since vagueness of this kind is, according to their arguments, an essential feature of languages used by creatures with our perceptual limitations, as well as an inevitable source of incoherence, there appears to be no way out of the problem. I look at some recent attempts to resolve this dilemma in chapter 5. In chapter 6 I develop a new approach to the Sorites. It provides a way out of the paradox which is sensitive to the considerations Dummett and Wright discuss and makes it possible to justify the linguistic behaviour of language users as based on coherent principles. In chapter 7 I discuss a number of problems for this approach and in chapter 8 consider some related difficulties to do with visual perception. In the final chapter I relate this solution to Dummett's and Wright's arguments. I also argue there that an adequate approach to vagueness should respect the context-dependence of observational predicates and sketch a development of the framework Lewis provides in *Convention* to accomode this feature of natural languages.

I would like to here acknowledge the support of various friends and colleagues who have made this project possible. I am very grateful to Allen Hazen, Brenda Judge, Errol Martin, Denis Robinson and Barry Taylor for their helpful comments on earlier drafts of this work and for useful discussion of the problems investigated in it.

I would also like to thank David Davenport, Pam Davoren, Beatrice Hamilton, Pat Johnson, Ailsa MacKenzie, Len O'Neill, Rosemary Smith and Jan Srzednicki for encouragement and help of various kinds, without which this book could not have been completed.

Part I:

PUZZLES, PROBLEMS AND PARADOXES

Chapter One

CONCEPTIONS OF VAGUENESS

1.1 Frege's Metaphor and The Sorites Paradox

Vagueness is not easy to characterize or define. One reason for this difficulty is that there appears to be a number of different conceptions of vagueness, and it is not clear just what they have in common. An intuitive grasp of one conception of vagueness may, however, be provided at this point by considering a metaphor Frege uses in his *Grundgesetze der Arithmetic*. He writes:[1]

> A definition of a concept (of a possible predicate) must be complete; it must unambiguously determine, as regards any object, whether or not it falls under the concept (whether or not the predicate is truly assertible of it). Thus there must not be any object as regards which the definition leaves in doubt whether it falls under the concept... We may express this metaphorically as follows: the concept must have a sharp boundary. To a concept without a sharp boundary there would correspond an area that had not a sharp boundary-line all around, but in places just vaguely faded away into the background.

This spatial metaphor provides a clear contrast between vague and precise concepts and terms. A non-vague term is one which is sharply defined in the sense that it neatly divides objects into those contained in the term's extension and those contained in the extension of its negation. A vague term is one whose correct definition permits the possibility of borderline cases. These are cases where it is not determined whether or not the term applies or fails to apply. Where there is vagueness there is genuine uncertainty concerning the application of expressions to certain objects.

---

1 Geach and Black [1], p.159.

Frege recognized that many ordinary concepts and predicates of natural language lack definitions which sharply determine their application in every case. His remarks about them perhaps leave open the possibility that these expressions lack complete definitions as a matter of fact (i.e. because no one has bothered to supply any yet): alternatively his remarks might be interpreted as compatible with the view that where a term is vague no correct set of complete application conditions could be given. I will argue for the second view of vagueness, as due not to a mere oversight which could be remedied, but to ineliminable aspects of natural language.

The existence in language of vagueness of this sort is regarded by Frege as a defect. "A concept that is not sharply defined is wrongly termed a concept" he claims.[2] He gives two reasons for dismissing these quasi-conceptual constructions: they lack meaning (Bedeutung), and the laws of logic fail when applied to them. On Frege's view any systematic theory of meaning must assign unique elements as semantic values to each significant linguistic unit. The significance of complex sentences is determined by the significance of their parts. Since no unique set of things can serve as the semantic value of a vague predicate, vagueness would have to be eliminated from a language before any systematic account of it could be given. Vagueness amounts to incoherence. His second reason for thinking this was that he saw the existence of borderline cases of the application of an expression as a threat to laws of classical logic, such as the Law of Excluded Middle (ExM): the principle that, for any statement P, either P or else -P. This principle seems under threat where the statement P consists of an application of a vague predicate to an object on the border of the predicate's scope. Frege thought, moreover, that no set of precise logical principles could represent the workings of a vague language; this is the force of his claim that vagueness amounts to incoherence.

It is not clear however, that ExM does fail in those cases where there is uncertainty about the truth of the disjuncts. (This is an issue we discuss in section 3.2.) But even if it is decided, on the strength of the existence of borderline cases, that ExM ought to be rejected, then these considerations cannot, on their own, establish that *no* set of precise principles could qualify as the logic of a vague language. (In chapter 3 we consider some non-classical alternatives.) Frege's first reason for regarding

---

2 Geach and Black [1], p.159.

vagueness as a defect does not seem adequate either. Ordinary predicates which lack definitions which are complete in his sense are understood as well as any others. It seems that meaning ought not to be divorced from understanding for when someone understands an expression what is grasped, surely, is its meaning. So from this point of view Frege's reasons for thinking that vagueness introduces incoherence (lack of sense) seem unsatisfactory.

There is, however, a stronger reason for thinking that Frege might have been right. For incoherence is a source of paradox, and there appears to be a close connexion between vagueness of the kind he describes and the Sorites Paradox. If the applicability of many ordinary predicates fades off imperceptibly, as his metaphor suggests, then there are no clear limits to their scope. There can be no definite answer then to questions about exactly where the correct application of the predicate ends and where the scope of its negation begins. To draw a boundary-line at any point to delimit the scope of such a predicate would not just be arbitrary: it would involve ignoring the fact that the predicate is genuinely vague in the way Frege depicts. It would be to treat it as like any sharply defined predicate. But if we are not permitted to draw limits to a predicate's application at any point, then there is no stopping its indiscriminate spread.

Granting this, the paradox inevitable. Suppose the predicate "heap" is vague in this Fregean sense. A series of things could be arranged in such a way that the first consists of a large heap of grains of some kind and each subsequent member consists of grains of the same kind but contains, in each case, one less grain than the one before. (Alternatively, the series could consist of temporal stages of a single object which is a heap at the first stage and has one less grain at each succeeding stage.) The last member, which consists of a single grain, is obviously not a heap. But if any member of the series is a heap, then it would surely remain so if just one grain were subtracted. The application conditions for the predicate are not sharp enough to distinguish heaps from non-heaps on the basis of the difference of a single grain so if one member of a (suitably gradated) series is a heap, so is the next. Since the first member is certainly a heap, all the subsequent members are also, including the last. To deny this would involve supposing that a sharp boundary can be drawn at some point to divide the heaps from the non-heaps. But this would amount to a denial that the predicate is vague in the way Frege depicts.

It might be argued on these grounds that Frege was right in thinking that the presence of vagueness in a language renders it incoherent.

Since Frege most of the debates about vagueness have consisted of alternative proposals for dealing with the paradox just outlined. Some favour modifications to orthodox logic and others reform of semantic theory. Versions of each of these alternatives will be discussed in chapter 3. It is argued there that the attempted solutions offered by fuzzy logics and supervaluation systems consists in 'precisifying away' vagueness of the kind with which Frege was concerned. But the puzzle only arises if there is vagueness of this kind in language: it is not to be solved by ignoring its existence.

The consequences of admitting that natural language is vague in the sense Frege specified will be discussed in the second part of the book. In chapter 4 I shall discuss a radical view of the paradox to be found in the writings of Michael Dummett and Crispin Wright. They argue that if vagueness is taken seriously, the Sorites turns out to be a genuine irresolvable paradox: no logic or consistent set of semantic principles could adequately represent the workings of a vague language. Dummett and Wright argue that, for this reason, Frege's pessimism about the possibility of providing a precise account of natural language is vindicated. They disagree, however, with his view of vagueness as a mere defect of those languages to be eliminated before the task of providing a satisfactory account of them can be started. If their arguments (to be discussed in detail in subsequent chapters) are correct, then vagueness must be regarded as an essential feature of natural languages, a feature which is not to be ignored or precisified away by an adequate account of their workings. The conclusion of these arguments is that vagueness is both an essential feature of natural languages and an incoherent one: it is a source of contradictions and paradox, but it cannot be eliminated. The paradox may be dissolved and language made to appear in perfect working order but only at the expense of treating vagueness as if it did not exist. If, on the other hand, vagueness is taken seriously it would follow on this argument that no coherent theory of the workings of natural language is possible.

Neither Dummett nor Wright seems willing to accept the conclusion of these arguments but it is not clear in either case where they think it ought to be challenged. Dummett locates the source of the dilemma in a tension between the views of language held by Wittgenstein and by Frege. He writes:[3]

> A satisfactory account of vagueness ought to explain two contrary feelings that we have: that expressed by Frege that the presence of vague expressions in a language invests it with an intrinsic incoherence: and the opposite point of view contended for by Wittgenstein, that vagueness is an essential feature of language.

The dilemma must be resolved however, for it is clear that the conclusions outlined above cannot be accepted. The motivation for the philosophical study of natural languages surely consists in the desire to make sense of the workings of those languages and so to dissolve paradoxes to which they appear to lead. The idea that ordinary languages are massively incoherent is incompatible with their communicative function and with the degree of regularity evident in their use. And so the main project undertaken here will be to argue that the coherence of natural languages may be reconciled with their vagueness.

Dummett's and Wright's arguments are discussed in detail in chapter 4, and in chapter 5 some attempts to resolve the Sorites Paradox are discussed and found to be inadequate. In the chapters that follow a solution is found to this dilemma and to the Sorites Paradox, and some of its consequences are investigated.

1.2 The Vehicle of Vagueness

One of the reasons why vagueness is not easy to characterize or define may be seen by considering the range of things which may be claimed to be vague and the debates about the nature of the vagueness in each case.

(a) Vagueness is usually taken to be a linguistic phenomenon: a semantic property of *types of expression* of natural language.

Most philosophers agree with Frege's view of it as a defect of those languages. Kit Fine describes it as a "deficiency of meaning" (Fine [1], p.268). It must be distinguished, he says, from other semantic defects. Remarks which are obscure,

---

3 Dummett [1], p.312.

ambiguous or highly unspecific might be considered defective because of indefiniteness about the meanings of expressions they contain. Fine thinks a sharp line can be drawn between these varieties of indefiniteness and vagueness. All vagueness reduces, he claims, to the vagueness of predicates. A predicate is vague when its meaning fails to determine whether or not it applies in certain (at least possible) cases. Sentences are vague when they contain vague terms.

Genuine vagueness concerning the application of predicates is usually distinguished from mere uncertainty about their scope due to ignorance of deciding facts. Haack, in *Deviant Logic*, distinguishes two ways in which uncertainty about the application of a predicate can arise:

(i) the qualifications for being F are imprecise:
(ii) the qualifications for being F are precise, but there is difficulty in determining whether certain objects satisfy them.[4]

The latter epistemological variety of uncertainty may be due to inadequacy in measuring techniques or ignorance of the world. This is not genuine vagueness she says. Where there is genuine vagueness the uncertainty is not to be resolved by further investigation of the world. So where F is a vague predicate there are (or at least could be) objects of which it cannot be decided whether or not they belong within the extension of F, not just because we lack the practical means of determining the question, but because there is no right answer.

One reason for the prevalence of borderline cases of the application of observational predicates is the existence of continua of various sorts in nature: we are sometimes faced with a range of cases where a predicate clearly applies at one end and certainly fails to apply at the other but it is not at all clear what ought to be said about the cases in between. Borderline cases of a predicate's application seem bound to occur whenever this situation can arise, that is wherever there can be a sequence of objects displaying gradual variation from paradigm cases of the application of the observational predicate at one end to clear instances of its non-application at the other. For the linguistic dispositions of speakers do not determine sharp limits to the scope of such predicates as "red", "pink" and "orange" and

---

4 Haack [1], p.110.

"tall"and "short" which apply to things which can be placed on various continua of this sort.

It is sometimes thought that this variety of uncertainty due to vagueness might nevertheless be eliminated by total knowledge of the dispositions of users of the language. Though the qualifications for being F which are known to the ordinary users of the language are imprecise, linguistic facts about those users might be thought to decide all questions about whether particular objects are within the scope of application of F or not. This raises issues to be discussed in chapter 2 concerning the relation between linguistic behaviour of a population and the semantic properties of the language they speak. We shall argue there that facts about linguistic behaviour do not resolve the uncertainty concerning the application of some natural language predicates, and so there is a case for saying that they are genuinely vague in Frege's and Fine's semantic sense.

(b) Some have claimed, on the other hand, that it is *uses of language* which are properly said to be vague.

Vagueness is a pragmatic matter, on this view. "A word which is actually used in a fluctuating way (such as "heap" or "pink") is..vague" (Waismann [1], p.38). "Languages themselves are free of vagueness but the linguistic conventions of a population or the linguistic habits of a person select not a point but a fuzzy region in the space of precise languages" (Lewis [2], p.64). On Lewis's view there need be no vagueness about meanings. Meanings may be regarded as functions which make assignments to strings of marks and sounds: truth-values in the case of sentences, objects for names and so on. Psychological and sociological facts determine which of these abstract semantic systems is actually used by a person or a community, and vagueness exists where there is a multiplicity of alternative precise languages available to speakers in a community.

It is natural to ask what the relation might be between these precise languages and psychological reality. Why should a speaker's linguistic habits be indeterminate? Answers might be sought either in vagueness in psychological phenomena (a suggestion we consider briefly in the next subsection) or in the social contingencies of language learning and communication.

Many of those who take vagueness to consist in fluctuations in usage offer quite different accounts to Lewis's, often influenced by Wittgenstein's remarks on vagueness in his *Philosophical*

Investigations. Wittgenstein rejects there Frege's view of the way language works and the nature of meaning. Words acquire meaning and reference by our use of them and where that use fails to fully determine meanings the result will be uncertainty concerning the range of application of a word. Actual usage is restricted to a limited range of circumstances and guided by particular interests and purposes and there is no saying how it would extend to further unconsidered circumstances. Wittgenstein agrees therefore with Frege that there are no rigid boundaries to ordinary concepts such as that of Christianity, or a game, or greenness and no answers to what counts as within the extension of a term and what no longer qualifies. But since we understand these vague terms perfectly well and there is nothing defective about their meaning, Frege's views about meaning cannot be right.

Why then do we find ourselves in this position of understanding vague concepts but being unable to say where they are bounded? Wittgenstein's answer is connected with his views on rule-following and what is involved in understanding the meaning of a word His negative remarks on what is not involved in understanding vague concepts are clear: grasping the sense of a word cannot be a matter of coming to possess a rule which unambiguously determines its application in all cases, nor is it like acquiring a picture or template in the mind. If it was the latter we would not be at a loss when asked to say exactly which shape is the shape of a leaf, or which precise shade of green is my idea of greenness. Nor is it a matter of having a definition in mind or a description of the thing defined. He uses the example here of a speaker who makes a meaningful statement about Moses but who has no ready definition or description of who they mean which could deal with all contingencies. If some parts of the story about Moses are proven false it is not certain whether "Moses existed" would remain true for the speaker: they have not decided beforehand how much and which parts of the story are essential.

The positive remarks about what is involved in understanding a vague term are less clear. If someone is explaining what a game is they are likely to provide a few examples known to the audience and then say something like, "These and similar things are called games". The speaker intends the examples to be taken in a particular way and they usually are: training of this sort is mostly successful. A speaker's understanding of a word like "green" may be explained in terms of their having grasped a schema and its meaning, taught with the use of colour samples, but only if the schema or sample is understood in a certain way: it must be understood *as* a schema or general sample, not as an individual shade. It is useful to the learner only if they grasp the way others would use it and thereby grasp the rough range of similarity of shade to this which still counts as green. Similarly, a speaker may be able to produce some description of who they mean by Moses but this description does not even approximate Frege's strict definitions which unambiguously and uniquely determine the applicability of the expression.

The reason why understanding a vague word does not equip us with rules for using it on every conceivable occasion is that the rules we follow in applying it are themselves vague. Vague rules are indefinite ones; they include instructions of a kind which might be used to teach the meaning of a word like "game", or "green", such as "Things like this are green", "These and similar things are games", etc. The scope for alternative interpretations of such rules can never be excluded, and so there are bound to be borderline cases. So the meanings of these sentences are vague in this sense of being able to be understood in a number of ways: they remain perfectly in order however.

In his book on Wittgenstein Kripke suggests at one point[5] that Wittgenstein is more concerned with the ordinary conception of vagueness than the borderline case one which has interested most philosophers. But if the above suggestions about the meaning of his remarks about vague rules is correct Wittgenstein's account may be understood as an explanation of the prevalence of vagueness of the borderline case variety in language. Borderline cases arise because of essential features of human perception and language acquisition and use. Also, as we shall see shortly, it is not that easy to distinguish the two conceptions of vagueness sharply.

Despite some obscurity about his notion of grasping the indefinite meanings of vague terms and following vague rules, there is considerable plausibility in Wittgenstein's overall picture of the sources and nature of vagueness in language. We shall argue in later sections on the Sorites Paradox that some useful clues are to be found in Wittgenstein's notion of a vague rule and that it does illuminate one sources of borderline case vagueness in language.

---

5 Kripke [1], p.84.

(c) An investigation of the sources of vagueness in language or in linguistic habits of speakers may lead to the suggestion that *psychological phenomena* (thoughts, beliefs, perceptions, intentions etc.) may be vague also.

There do appear to be grounds for this view. Fine's example, "Casanova believes he has many mistresses" may be a vague report of a precise belief. But it may (as he points out) be a perfectly precise report of a vague belief (Fine [1], p.289). Indefiniteness of this sort in perceptions, memories, beliefs and intentions is sometimes described as vagueness. Russell develops this idea in the following way: "A memory is vague when it is appropriate to many different occurrences . A memory is precise when the occurrences that would verify it are narrowly circumscribed." (Russell [2], p.182). He takes the vagueness of psychological phenomena to be an instance of vagueness in representations. "A representation is vague when the relation of the representing system to the represented system is not one-one but one-many. For example a photograph which is so smudged that it might equally represent Brown or Jones or Robinson is vague. A small scale map is usually vaguer than a large scale map. Vagueness, clearly is a matter of degree, depending on the extent of the possible difference between different systems represented by the same representation. Accuracy, on the contrary, is an ideal limit". (Russell [1], p.85).

Russell's account of vagueness is not satisfactory since it runs together vagueness and generality. A memory may apply to a number of different incidents without being vague and it is hard to see why a representational system should be considered vague just because it contains one-many correspondences. If there is no uncertainty about what is representing what the system may be regarded as perfectly precise.

It does seem plausible, however, to suppose that psychological phenomena are sometimes vague in some sense. Freud, for example, takes vagueness to be a significant quality in dreams. He reports the following dream of his own of receiving a telegram from a friend in Italy:[6]

> "I saw it printed in blue on the telegram form. The first word was vague: 'via', perhaps, or 'villa' or possibly even 'casa':...each of the three alternatives

---

6 Freud [1], p.428.

> for the first word turned out on analysis to be an independent and equally valid starting point for a chain of thoughts."

Dreams show a tendency to condense and combine alternatives into a single representation. They are said for this reason to be obscure and indefinite for there is often no single correct answer to questions about their content. Freud treats these occurrences of vagueness as especially important since he takes the work of condensation and the resulting obscurity to be motivated by tendencies to repress and censor some of the condensed features.

Vagueness of this same kind in other psychological phenomena may be motivated by different concerns. Indefiniteness of this variety in beliefs and perceptions seems due often to the need for economical encoding of information. What is noticed, perceived or remembered of a situation often glosses over the specific details which distinguish that situation from others similar with respect to the features taken to be important by an observer. The reasons for this economy are obvious: "photographic" memories would be unmanageable, unselective perceptions a useless burden. But since it is the specific details which distinguish one possible situation from others the result of this economy may be vagueness. It is only called vagueness when it is inconvenient however: the testimony of the observer in the witness box is likely to be criticised as too vague only when the witness is unable to recall details of a scene which the jury take to be vital.

The phenomenon of indefiniteness in perception is a fertile source of puzzles and paradoxes.[7] The failure of intersubstitutivity of different descriptions of an object seen or thought of is due often to indefiniteness of the perception or thought. Indefiniteness in beliefs is often the cause of failure of substitutions to preserve truth-values in the linguistic contexts of belief reports and where the belief concerns the speaker's immediate environment it is likely to be caused by an indefinite perception, that is, one which does not discriminate between distinct visual possibilities.

Other puzzles are produced by phenomena which admit of distinct interpretations. Pictures which present two or more aspects (such as Necker cubes and some of Escher's drawings)

---

7 See Anscombe, "The Intentionality of Sensation", in Butler [1], for a discussion of some of these puzzles

provide examples of representations which can be seen in distinct ways. There are many other more ordinary cases of indefiniteness in perception: the seeing of an indefinite number of leaves on a tree or people in a crowded street are obvious instances. One particularly interesting puzzle for the discussion of the Sorites concerns the perception of triads of coloured objects whose first and third members look just discernibly different in colour to an observer but whose second member is perceived by the observer to be not definitely discriminable in shade from the ones on either side. In chapter 8 we discuss the relation between these puzzles and the Sorites.

The variety of vagueness or potential for creating vagueness evident in these cases of indefiniteness in dreams, memories, beliefs and perceptions appears to have little to do with the existence of borderline cases. Russell's account of the kind of vagueness involved is not satisfactory but some detailed account which does succeed in distinguishing vagueness from generality is required. It seems evident that what should distinguish the two is the kind of non-epistemic uncertainty which is produced by genuine cases of vagueness. In each of the cases discussed above it is the potential for creating uncertainty about the content or reference of the representation which makes it natural to describe it as vague.

(d) It has sometimes been suggested that *objects, events or states of affairs in the world* may be vague.

This suggestion is usually raised only to be rejected. "Against this no more can be said except that it is obvious that to be is to be determinate" (Armstrong [1], p.220). Dummett ([1], p.314) writes: "The notion that things might actually be vague, as well as being vaguely described, is not properly intelligible" . Dummett has second thoughts on this matter however, and later describes the view that there can be no vagueness in nature as "a deep, but unwarranted philosophical predudice" (Dummett [2], p.9).

It does seem possible to find an intelligible sense in which things may be vague. Dummett in [2] suggests that it would make sense to suppose this was so if we were forced to conclude that the world or some objects in it could only be described by a vague language. If there is irremediable uncertainty about the spatial boundaries of some objects or about their temporal extent, uncertainty which is not to be eliminated by any possible empirical investigation, then there would seem to be a good sense in which there is vagueness in nature.

Evans argues against the coherence of this conception in "Can There Be Vague Objects?" (Evans [1]) on the grounds that to suppose there could be indeterminate identity statements conflicts with Leibniz's Law. Where 'a' and 'b' are singular terms such that 'a=b' is indeterminate in truth-value ('Ind(a=b'), we may conclude concerning b, that

$$\hat{x}[\mathrm{Ind}(x=a)]b.$$

But since

$$-\mathrm{Ind}(a=a),$$

and so

$$-\hat{x}[\mathrm{Ind}(x=a)]a,$$

Leibniz's Law may be used to conclude that

$$-(a=b),$$

contradicting the assumption with which we began.

But haziness about the boundaries of an object should not throw any doubt on identity statements concerning it. Where 'a' and 'b' name the same hazy object, the indefiniteness of its boundaries is no grounds for supposing the identity statement is vague or indefinite in truth-value. On the other hand, where one of the labels 'a' or 'b' denotes an object with sharply delimited boundaries and the other, one with hazy boundaries, then it might be thought that (a=b) is indefinite, on the grounds that it is uncertain whether or not a and b coincide. But this cannot be right. For suppose 'a' denotes a certain determinate set of molecules and 'b' is the name of a cloud of gas of uncertain extent. The relation between a and b cannot be that of identity since it is not transitive: some sharply delimited object c might be as good a candidate as a for identity with b, but it is definitely not the case that (a=c). It is false therefore rather than indeterminate that (a=b), for no hazily bounded object can be identical with a precisely bounded one if identity is to be a transitive relation.

So Evans's argument does not appear to undermine the coherence of this conception of vagueness. For the vagueness, in Dummett's sense, of certain objects need not mean that any identity statements are vague.

Our main concern from here on will be with borderline case vagueness in language and hence with the kinds of views expressed in 1.2(a) and 1.2(b). But it is possible to discern one feature which seems to be possessed by both linguistic and non-linguistic cases of vagueness: where there is genuine vagueness there appears to be scope for uncertainty of some kind which is non-epistemic. Just as vagueness of a semantic kind in expression types or uncertainty in a speaker's linguistic habits can generate a class of borderline case objects, so indefiniteness in psychological phenomena constitutes vagueness when it produces uncertainty, as does indefiniteness about the spatial and temporal borders of objects where it is not of a kind which can be remedied by further investigation of the world.

1.3 Something Else to do with Vagueness

The range of the views discussed in the last section makes it plausible to suppose that there is more than one variety of vagueness but it is not at all clear what the differences between them might be or how the different kinds of vagueness in language might be characterized. It is at least clear that in all the cases discussed above genuine vagueness is a source of uncertainty of a kind which is not to be eliminated by empirical investigation. It is also commonly supposed by philosophers that it is possible to distinguish at least two distinct conceptions of vagueness. The first sort is *borderline case* vagueness in language, of the kind defined by Frege and Fine, which is regarded as the source of interesting problems and puzzles such as the Sorites. The second, which might be called *indefiniteness*, is to be found in psychological phenomena as well as in language. In the first case the uncertainty concerns the fringes of application of a word. In the second it is due to indefiniteness about the actual content of a concept or representation. There is indefiniteness of this latter sort where there is irremediable uncertainty concerning which or how many of a number of things or what range of things of a certain kind are being represented in thought or encompassed by the meaning of a term. This conception of vagueness appears to be distinct from the borderline case conception.

It is often denied that this notion of "glossing over distinguishable options" is a genuine variety of vagueness at all. It is hard to see however why it might be maintained that the title of this section was not vague, unless it was by a philosopher concerned to restrict vagueness to the borderline case variety narrowly conceived.

The usual way in which borderline case vagueness is conceived is too narrow as an account of all vagueness in language. The sense in which the title of this section is vague and in which remarks made in ordinary conversations are sometimes criticised as being "too vague" does not appear to have much to do with the potential of contained expressions for generating borderline cases. It is not the presence of words having borderline cases which leads us to stigmatize sentences as vague in ordinary conversations. Sentences which are criticised for this reason are usually ones which fail to meet expectations set up in some way by the contexts in which they are uttered. It is the failure to provide much specific information which leads an audience to reject such a statement as vague, rather than the potential of contained expressions for generating borderline cases. Sentences which manage, without being ambiguous, to admit of a variety of diverse interpretations are often rejected as vague for this reason. ("Mary is a nice girl" might be an example of this.)

Whether or not the statement counts as vague depends, however, on the audience's expectations. President Bush's announcement that he will defend American interests in Nicaragua counts as vague if what is wanted is definite and useful information about current American foreign policy. In other contexts it may pass as non-vague. Vagueness of this sort is a well-known strategy for telling the truth without giving much away. Opposing "unnecessary and excessive spending" will alienate no voters; cuts in social services will. As Jerry Brown remarked when governor of California, "In politics a little vagueness goes a long way".

Though most philosophers who have written on vagueness share Fine's conception of the subject it is clear that the vagueness of sentences is not always due simply to their containing predicates which may have borderline cases. As well as being too narrow as an account of all there is to vagueness in language the borderline case conception as stated by Fine also seems too *wide*. It counts as vague such sentences as "Peter Garrett is bald" and "British postboxes are red" which would not normally be considered vague. They do, however, contain predicates which have borderline cases and would be considered vague for this reason on Fine's version of the borderline case conception.

Vagueness of the ordinary kind (described above as indefiniteness) should not be identified with borderline case vagueness.

For suppose that a program of precisification was carried out (of the sort some philosophers have recommended) and all vagueness of the borderline case kind was eliminated from the language. Limits to the application of words such as "red", "tall", "bald" and so on are laid down so that all objects are divided into those that fall under them and those that do not. It is clear that there would still be scope for vagueness of the other sort in language. A precise diplomatic code book, laying down the alternative actions which constitute "strong opposition" will still allow for a dimension of vagueness so long as there are distinct alternatives to be glossed over. ("Strong opposition" might, for instance, cover economic embargos as well as the declaration of war and use of nuclear weapons.) Since indefiniteness in sentences is compatible with precise cut-off points in the application of contained expressions it seems that it must be distinguished from borderline case vagueness.

If this is so the conclusion must be that there are at least two dimensions of vagueness in language. It seems necessary to admit both sorts to accommodate our intuitions about vagueness. The way in which instances of vagueness are thought to generate uncertainty over the Law of Excluded Middle and the Principle of Bivalence may be explained if these instances are taken to be cases of vagueness of the borderline case kind. But the vagueness in the other sense of most psychological phenomena and many sentences is also evident to everyone. It is a commonplace that vagueness comes in degrees and the vaguer a statement is the better its chances of being true and the less information it conveys. This is explicable on the second conception of vagueness for the greater the range of distinct possible states of affairs glossed over by a vague statement the more likely it is that the actual state of affairs is amongst them. But on the borderline case conception a statement is vague just if it contains some expressions which have borderline cases.

Both dimensions of vagueness may be discerned in certain expressions of natural language. A statement such as "London is a large city", which is clearly true, can be said to be vague in the borderline case sense since there are borderline cases of large cities. It is neither more nor less vague in this sense than most other statements. It also seems to be vague by comparison with a statement specifying the exact population of London. Also, expressions such as "many" and "a few", which appear to be quantifiers, are vague in that there may be borderline cases of many things (of some sort) or of a few things (of a sort): cases where it is uncertain whether it is correct or not to make use of the term in the description of some situation. But these terms exhibit another, perhaps (in some sense) more basic, dimension of vagueness in that an assertion that there are many Xs present or that a few of the Ys are Z leaves it unclear (i.e. it is an indefinite matter) just how many Xs there are or how many of the Ys are Z. This kind of vagueness is to be found in clear and central cases of the application of these terms.

Unfortunately the situation is not as tidy as this account suggests. For no very sharp line can be drawn between vagueness of the ordinary (non-borderline case) kind and the other semantic defects Fine mentions. Philosophers often criticize as vague remarks whose fault is considered to be obscurity of some kind. Unclarity, lack of specificity and the glossing over of distinctions considered important by the critic are usually stigmatized as vaguenesses.[8] Some have insisted that these faults should be distinguished sharply from vagueness. Alston says that although the word "vague" is often used very loosely to apply to any kind of indeterminacy, unclarity or lack of specificity this is simply a mistake. A term is only properly said to be vague when there are cases in which no definite answer can be given to the question of whether or not it applies.[9] It emerges however, from what Alston goes on to say and from Fine's remarks, that this uncertainty about the fringes of a word's application is to be blamed on an indefiniteness, in the sense of lack of specificity, about its meaning. So rather than seeing just one variety of genuine vagueness, defined in terms of borderline cases, or two distinct notions (the "ordinary" and the borderline case variety), it seems better to see the situation as one in which there is a cluster of related notions including obscurity, lack of specificity, lack of informativeness and hazy boundaries of application. Vagueness exists where these generate a certain kind of non-epistemic uncertainty.

So although eliminating borderline case vagueness in language (were such a project feasible) would leave vagueness of other varieties untouched, there appear to be important connexions between the various kinds of vagueness and no very sharp distinctions between them. Fine's and Frege's accounts of

---

8 For a few examples see Davies [1], pp.8, 10, 41, 44, 45, 54; Loar, in Evans and McDowell [1], p.142; Platts [1], pp.45 and 62; and Taylor, in Evans and McDowell [1], p.263.

9 Alston [1], pp.84f.

borderline case vagueness in predicates blames it on vagueness in meanings and this kind of vagueness appears to be a variety of indefiniteness. Vague concepts, on Frege's view, may be seen as sliding between alternative sharp definitions: and on Fine's account the intension of a vague predicate determines a range of distinct extensions, no one of which can definitely be identified as *the* extension of the predicate. Uncertainty about the fringes of application of a word is a consequence of its sense not being fully determinate. It is not clear, however, what can be made of this notion of indefinite meanings on current accounts of meaning. We discuss some approaches to this problem in sections of various chapters to follow and shall make some suggestions about the relation between the two kinds of vagueness in the final section of the last chapter. In the remainder of this chapter we shall consider in more detail the borderline case conception of vagueness.

1.4 Intensional and Extensional Vagueness

Fine distinguishes an intensional and extensional sense of vagueness corresponding to the intensional and extensional conception of meaning (Fine [1], p.266). In a world in which everyone were either uniformly hirsute or else completely hairless the predicate "bald" could remain vague in the intensional sense: the sense in which the meaning of the predicate permits the possibility of borderline cases. To be extensionally vague, on the other hand, a term must have actual borderline cases.

This view of vagueness comes from Carnap's account of the analysis of meaning in "Meaning and Synonymy in Natural Languages" (Carnap [1], pp.233f.). He suggests an empirical method for determining the extensions and intensions of observational predicates of natural languages. On the basis of observations of a language user's utterances a linguist decides whether or not they are willing to apply a predicate to given things within a certain region. This fixes the extension of the predicate within that region, the extension of its contradictory and the intermediate class of things for which the person is not willing to either affirm or deny the predicate. The existence of the third class of things marks the extensional vagueness of observational predicates. The linguist can then formulate inductive hypotheses about the the language user's responses to things outside this limited region.

Hypotheses concerning the intensions of observational predicates are also, Carnap claims, empirical ones which can be tested. They are to be tested by asking the person how they would classify possible non-actual cases which can be described or pictured. The linguist's aim in investigating intensions is to determine the range of variation in relevant respects from actual items which would still fall within the scope of the predicate. Carnap claims this range is not clearly delimited since to determine it the linguist must pose questions the language user will not have considered before and to which they may have no answers ready. Thus there will be a range of intensional vagueness also.

It is clear that it is this intensional variety of vagueness with which Fine, Frege and most other philosophers have been concerned. For vagueness is, in their view, a semantic defect of natural languages, and it seems wrong to make the question of whether or not a term is vague depend on what happens to be the case in the world. And it is the intensional sense of meaning with which most semantic theorists have been concerned. There is a further reason for restricting attention to the intensional conception of vagueness. It is generally agreed that Sorites arguments are a genuine source of puzzles and paradoxes which have to do with vagueness and the vagueness involved here is of the intensional sort. A policy of eliminating existing borderline cases would surely not eliminate the Sorites paradox. Even if such a policy were successfully carried out and all candidates for some particular intermediate position or positions in a Sorites series were destroyed, concern about the paradox could be revived by considering the possibility that objects filling those positions could come into existence again at any time in the future.

This dependence of the paradox on the intensional conception of borderline case vagueness appears clearly, for example, in Unger's version. (See Unger [1] or [2].) This version involves considering any normal middle-sized object - such as an adult wombat for instance - and imagining that single atoms are ticked off it one at a time in the most innocuous way possible until there is nothing left. Unger's claim is that at no point is there a sudden transition from there being a wombat at one stage to there being no wombat at the next. He admits that it may not be technically possible to carry out the envisaged process and it is even possible that no orderly series of stages exhibiting the transition has existed. Still, the Unger version is a genuine paradox. And so we will be concerned with the intensional variety of vagueness from here on.

1.5 Commitments

Scheffler claims[10] that a borderline case conception of vagueness need not be committed to the existence of possible entities. The term "cat" could be vague in this sense, even if no borderline cases of cats existed in the animal realm, for a linguist assessing intensional vagueness using Carnap's method could draw bizarre pictures of felinelike creatures or make up actual descriptions of a science fiction sort to test language users' dispositions. Where the question "Is this a cat?" is undecidable the term is vague. But Scheffler's approach hardly avoids problems to do with possibilia since it makes use of possible representations and counterfactuals. A term is vague on his view if language users would respond in this way were they presented with such representations.

It seems necessary in any discussion of semantics generally, and in considering puzzles to do with vagueness in particular, to make sense of talk of possible entities, meanings, expression-types and necessity. The preservation of anything resembling our prephilosophical notion of meaning requires some kind of intensional entities such as possibilia or propositional entities. Any attempt to resolve problems inherent in the conceptual apparatus necessary for an adequately rich account of the nature of language and its relation to thought and the world must assume that the task of making sense of these notions can be successfully completed. The best attempts so far make use of possible world semantics[11] but it would be beyond the scope of the present essay to consider the advantages of the various alternatives. So we shall assume from here on that any philosophical qualms concerning the commitments incurred so far can be resolved.

The borderline case conception of vagueness also carries a commitment to the analytic/synthetic distinction. This is taken on with Haack's distinction between epistemic uncertainty concerning the truth-value of a statement and semantic uncertainty due to vagueness. For the claim is that vague predicates are ones whose applicability to certain objects could not be settled by any possible investigation of the empirical facts. The claim rests on the assumption that it is possible to distinguish in some non-question begging way between matters which are determined by the facts and those which are not. This appears to involve a rejection of Quine's view that no statement is immune from

[10] Scheffler [1], ch.3.

[11] See Cresswell [1], and Lewis [1] and [2].

revision in the light of further investigation of the world.[12] There seems, however, notwithstanding Quine's claims, to be a genuine difference here: a difference between cases where the truth-value of a statement is unknown due to ignorance of the relevant facts and situations where no further investigation of the world would resolve our doubts. We are able to distinguish ignorance from vagueness.

It could be argued, however, in support of Quine's view, that situations can easily be imagined where observations of the world would resolve questions about the truth-value of vague statements. Where the truth-value of "Fa" is uncertain because a is a borderline case of F-hood the issue could be resolved if the dispute mattered enough to lead the interested parties to agree upon a stipulation sharpening the conditions for the application of the predicate. *Ad hoc* decisions seem appropriate in such cases, and the parties need not entertain any intention of permanently altering their speech habits or those of the community at large. No change of meaning is envisaged and it does not appear to conflict seriously with the meanings of vague terms to adopt such policies in particular contexts.

Lakatos has argued persuasively in another context[13] that it is possible to single out particular situations as especially germane to the truth or falsehood of a given statement relative to a set of decisions about background assumptions. Once it is decided what is to be taken for granted (for the moment at least), a statement's truth may be tested against the facts. It is usually clear in debates about a statement's truth-value what the accepted background assumptions are and so what might be decided on the basis of observation and what would remain an open question whatever was observed. Extra assumptions may always be explicitly introduced where it is thought worthwhile to do so and open questions settled by observation against this increased non-standard set of assumptions. (Sharp criteria in terms of wave-lengths of reflected light might, for example, be used to determine questions about the truth-values of statements predicating colour terms of their borderline cases.)

This situation will differ though, in certain clearly identifiable ways, from normal situations in which the facts decide an

---

12 It is usually truth, rather than lack of truth-value, which is thought by proponents of the analytic/synthetic distinction to depend in some cases on meaning and in others on fact.

13 Lakatos [1], pp.8f.

uncertain matter. Anyone not party to the agreed stipulation would not know which way the matter had been settled even if they were able to make all the same observations. And so we may say that there is genuine semantic indeterminacy where the truth-value of a statement can only be settled by explicitly introducing background assumptions additional to those normally taken for granted by users of the language. This is, of course, somewhat vague in the ordinary sense gestured towards in section 1.3 but it appears to have sufficient clarity to meet the difficulty at hand.

1.6 Fregean Vagueness

There is a stronger and a weaker version of the borderline case conception of vagueness. In the weak sense there is borderline case vagueness in a language just if it contains expressions which have or could have borderline cases. As well as the things which certainly belong in the extension of a vague term and those which definitely belong in its complement, there is a third class of things which do not definitely belong in either. On the stronger, or more radical, version of the borderline case conception the existence or potential for existence of such a third class of things is not sufficient to make a term genuinely vague. Vague terms, on this view, are ones whose sense is not such as to allow any clear dividing lines to be drawn between these three classes of things. So if, for example, the predicate "red" is vague in this stronger sense there is no saying where the cut-off point is between things which are red and things which are borderline cases of red. Nor is there any definite line to be drawn between borderline cases of redness and things which definitely do not deserve the predicate. Any lines drawn to demarcate these classes will be arbitrary divisions not determined by any language user's understanding of the sense of the predicate. Frege's picture of the applicability of a predicate gradually fading away is particularly appropriate to this version of the borderline case conception. We shall therefore refer to it as *boundary* or *Fregean vagueness*.

The question of whether expressions of natural language are vague in the Fregean sense or just in the weak sense is obviously important to the discussion of the problem outlined in section 1. For the Sorites Paradox only arises where there is Fregean vagueness. Weak borderline case vagueness in a predicate is compatible with the existence of sharp limits to the classes of things to which it correctly applies and things to which it is not correctly applied, for there may be a third, sharply delimited class of things of uncertain status. But if there is a right answer to the question of which member of a series is the last to which a predicate correctly applies there can be no grounds for the claim that if one member of the series deserves the predicate, so does the next. Borderline case vagueness would consist, on this view, just in the existence of truth-value gaps which may have sharply definable limits. The borderline cases begin and end at some definite, specifiable points. These might be impossible to specify in practice but the limits nevertheless exist where the term is vague only in this weak sense. So the Sorites Paradox is only worth considering seriously if the stronger Fregean type of vagueness also exists in language, for it is only then that it can be argued that the drawing of sharp limits to the scope of a predicate's application is unjustifiable.

Many of those who have discussed the borderline case conception of vagueness appear to have intended no more than the weak version. (See, for example, Alston's and Haack's definitions of vagueness in previous sections.) It may be doubted however that this is a genuine conception of vagueness. The question of whether the weak sense is a proper sense of vagueness arises because the existence of sharp limits to the class of borderline cases of a predicate's application means that there need be no irresolvable uncertainty or unclarity about the extent of its correct or definite application. Where there is a clearly delimited class of cases to which the term applies, another to which it does not apply, and a third sharply delimited class of neutral instances there seems to be no real uncertainty anywhere. The limits of the term's correct application, non-application and the neutral instances are perfectly clear. (Though there might be practical, empirical difficulties in determining them.) But as we argued in the last section, a term is only vague if there is genuine uncertainty about its application somewhere.

It could perhaps be replied to this argument that there is genuine uncertainty about the limits of application of predicates which are only weakly vague even though the class of borderline cases can be sharply delimited. For borderline cases are by their nature uncertain: neutral instances are cases of uncertain application. It might be argued that the right way of regarding the borderline cases of a predicate's application is as potential members of the extension of the predicate rather than as constituting a third category of genuinely neutral instances of its application. If the borderline cases are seen in this way there is genuine indeterminacy about where the limits of application of a weakly vague predicate are to be located. For there are a number of ways of drawing up definite boundaries to the application of such a predicate and so there will be a number of equally good contenders for the title of the "correct" extension of the predicate, each containing some, but not all, of the borderline cases. Since there is no way of deciding between them there is genuine uncertainty about the scope of the predicate's application. And so there is genuine vagueness.

The debate between these two versions of borderline case vagueness is often thought to depend upon whether or not there is higher order vagueness. Boundary vagueness is believed to exist only where there are borderline cases of borderline cases. It should not, however, be simply identified with higher order vagueness. The difference between the two will be discussed in section 3.5.

Whatever view is taken of higher order vagueness and of the propriety of calling the weak borderline case phenomenon genuine vagueness, a prior and more important issue concerning the existence of Fregean vagueness remains to be settled. The more important question, to which we now turn, is whether or not there is Fregean vagueness in language.

1.7 The Evidence for Fregean Vagueness

It appears from Carnap's precise account of the concept of vagueness that he has just the weaker variety in mind. He writes:

> In order to take vagueness into account, a pair of intensions F_1 and F_2 must be stated: X has the disposition of ascribing affirmatively the predicate 'Q' to an object y if and only if y has F_1; and the disposition of denying 'Q' for y if and only if y has F_2. Thus if y has neither F_1 nor F_2 X will give neither an affirmative nor a negative response; the property of having neither F_1 nor F_2 constitutes the zone of vagueness, which may possibly be empty.[14]

Vagueness exists then just where there is this third zone. These intensions must be stated in some language however, and so the possibility arises that the terms used to refer to F_1 and F_2 are themselves vague and that no more precise statement of the intension of Q is available in any language. For there may always be borderline cases of the application of the terms F_1 and F_2 to an

---

[14] Carnap [1], pp.242f.

object y. Also, if there is uncertainty on the part of a speaker of the kind Carnap describes, a linguist will be uncertain of the correct assignment of intensions to Q for that speaker. Since there will also be variation from speaker to speaker throughout the community there will be further uncertainty concerning the assignment of intensions to predicates of the language in general. For these reasons there is bound to be haziness about the scope of their correct application and about the limits of the class of their borderline cases. So it seems plausible to suppose that where vagueness of the kind Carnap describes is to be found in a natural language it will turn out to be Fregean vagueness.

We saw above that one reason for the prevalence of borderline cases of the application of observational predicates was the existence of continua. The linguistic dispositions of speakers do not determine sharp limits to the scope of predicates which apply to some of the things which can be placed on such continua. But neither do these dispositions determine sharp limits to the range of borderline cases of these predicates. Different members of a speech community would mark off different sections of such continua as delimiting the class of dubious cases and these alternative classifications would appear to be equally acceptable. These kinds of graduated sequences of objects may be easily imagined in the case of any predicate applied on the basis of casual observation, where judgements about a thing's sensory qualities depend just on how the thing looks, sounds, smells, tastes or otherwise strikes the senses on a single encounter. There may be alterations too gradual to be easily noticed in any of these dimensions of appearance, but the predicates are nevertheless applied just on the basis of casual observation, with no recourse to instruments or the past record of classification. To suppose that the boundaries of the borderline cases could somehow be sharply delimited on the basis of speakers' dispositions would be to deny that all this was so, for it would be to suppose that these dispositions determined a clearly correct answer in each case to the question of whether the predicate correctly applied, definitely failed to apply or neither. It would be to ignore the uncertainty, hedging and inconsistency which occurs from time to time in the responses of individual speakers and the variation from speaker to speaker which appears when they are asked to decide upon things towards the middle of continua of these kinds. So for these reasons there is bound to be uncertainty concerning the limits of the range of borderline cases.

Inconsistency is a prevalent feature of natural language. It may occur either between different language users' judgements, or between the judgements of a single language user at different times. Some competent users of the language will apply a predicate where others refuse to do so, and some will be willing to accept a predication in one context but not another. One person may judge a disputable object to be green while another, viewing it in the same lighting conditions and the same general context, claims it is blue.

Such discrepancies are regarded as unsurprising and are usually left unresolved, the parties agreeing to differ. They do not attract the kinds of strictures that are usually brought to bear on those who deviate from accepted usage. Provided the inconsistencies are confined within a certain range, they are not taken as reflecting on the competence of particular users. And so these observational predicates might be said to fit the world only loosely: individual applications of them may be inconsistent without being definitely unacceptable. Speakers are usually tolerant of conflicting judgements within this range, not bothering to resolve the discrepancy until practical difficulties force a choice. When a pair of speakers finds a discrepancy of this kind inconvenient they may agree to some *ad hoc* convention or stipulation designed to ensure agreement, usually regarding the choice of one rather than another resolution of the problem as an arbitrary matter.

The limits of the range of tolerated variation does not appear to be very clearly determined, since discrepancies may easily be imagined at a higher level if theorists who were also speakers of the language attempted to lay down definite boundaries to the area of permissible inconsistency. Inconsistency at this level between language-using theorists is evidence for the stronger variety of Fregean, or boundary, vagueness.

In general it seems that there will be vagueness in a predicate wherever it is possible to find suitable objects to fit onto every point in a sequence exhibiting degrees of justice with which the predicate could be applied. In some cases appropriate continua can actually be found: the work of wind and water on natural objects and processes of growth and decay in living things appears to provide examples of series of the kind required. Where continua do not occur naturally it seems at least possible that they could be arranged by selecting suitable intermediate objects to insert between the actual instances of the application of the predicate and the objects to which it clearly fails to apply.

Provided it is admitted that it is the intensional variety of vagueness with which we are concerned it seems that most ordinary predicates will be vague, for given any circumstance in which a predicate applies to an object with some degree of justice, it is always possible to imagine that object changing slightly, or being succeeded by another, so that there is fractionally more (or less) justice in applying the predicate to the new case. A term is intensionally vague if its meaning permits the possibility of borderline cases. And where there is intensional vagueness any attempt to draw a sharp, non-arbitrary line to delimit the class of borderline cases is bound to be defeated, for there is surely an inexhaustible supply of possible borderline cases. To suppose an intensionally vague predicate was only weakly vague, in that its meaning determined a natural category of borderline cases which could be sharply delimited from the clear cases of its application, would be to deny the possibility of discovering some further case, bordering on the boundary line, which could with equal justice be classified in either way. Given the infinite supply of possible borderline cases this threat to the clarity of dividing lines cannot be ignored.

One final reason for taking the borderline case vagueness of natural language to be vagueness of the stronger Fregean variety is provided by the evidence for the existence of open texture. Mastery of most ordinary terms is acquired in situations in which they are applied to a few salient objects from which the learner is prepared to extrapolate to some wider class of things. Colour terms and words like "person", "game", "dog", "tall" which are learned in this way, in connexion with paradigms or stereotypical objects, are said to have open texture in that the meaning they acquire in these contexts is not completely fixed and definite: it does not determine what should be said about cases which diverge from the paradigms in various ways. And it seems always possible, given any attempt to specify determinate conditions for the use of such a term, to imagine cases where there would be doubt about whether or not it applied.

Given the regularity evident in the use of language it seems inevitable that we see it as governed by rules, but the existence of open texture shows (as Waismann puts it) that we do not have rules ready for all imaginable circumstances.[15] The Wittgensteinian account of language sketched above may be used here to argue for the view that rules and definitions limit the

---

[15] Waismann [1], p.37.

scope of empirical concepts in some directions only and can never exclude an area of doubt. Even definitions in the natural sciences limit the scope of the meanings of terms for certain purposes only and for likely foreseeable circumstances. We must accept the fact that at present most empirical concepts can only be defined very vaguely.[16] The meaning of empirical terms may be sharpened at a later stage, but there is no saying *at present* which conceptual revisions and refinements are likely to prove useful.

If, as seems evident, natural languages do contain many terms which have open texture, the kind of vagueness to be found in them must be the Fregean variety. For where the applicability of a term is determined by speakers' recognition of loose similarities to paradigms and so cannot be captured by any set of precise rules, the set of borderline cases of its application cannot be sharply delimited. The situations in which these terms acquire meaning is such that their application is governed only by vague rules: rules which leave the competent user of the language without an adequate response in certain difficult cases. Just what the nature of such rules could be and how they differ from precise rules will be the topic of later sections.

---

16 Frege's picture of a set of clear 'central' cases surrounded by a fringe of dubious borderline cases does not seem complex enough to account for these sorts of examples of open texture. We could complicate it further in the way Kaplan suggests in his "Definition and the Specification of Meaning" (Kaplan [1], p.287) by introducing the notion of "indicators": descriptions of situations to which a term may be applied and which are introduced in a context in order to specify its meaning. In order to accommodate vagueness the specification of meaning for a term should, he claims, be understood in the following way:
the designation of a term should not in general be represented as a well-defined area, but as an open set of regions overlapping to a greater or lesser degree, each indicator determining one such region. The meaning of the term would correspond neither to the logical sum nor product of these regions, but to the pattern as a whole.

Chapter 2

LINGUISTIC BEHAVIOUR AND THE COMMUNAL LANGUAGE

The discussion of the previous chapter raises difficulties for various common assumptions about the nature of natural languages. It is often thought that though natural languages may be vague accounts of them need not be. It is assumed that it is possible to provide a precise semantic theory for a vague language.

Accounts of the relation between a formal language and the natural language for which it provides a model usually make use of Carnap's sense of *explication*. Explication is defined by Carnap as "making more precise a vague or not quite exact concept used in everyday life or in an earlier stage of scientific or logical development."[17] Explication in this sense obviously amounts to eliminating vagueness. But our interest is in vagueness and so a formal language could only provide an appropriate model of a vague natural language for our purposes if it did not eliminate its vagueness. It seems then that some relation other than explication would have to hold between the two if a formal language was to provide a model for a natural language which would be useful in giving an account of its vagueness. It is not clear what that relation could be.

In chapter 3 we investigate some ways of attempting to meet this problem, either by generalizing the set-theoretic apparatus or the semantic theory based upon it, in order to reflect the complexity of vague languages. Here we discuss some simpler moves which might seem to escape the difficulty altogether. They raise questions about the right account of the relation between linguistic behaviour and the communal language and present arguments that certain accounts of this relation can eliminate problems to do with vagueness at the level of semantic theory.

---

[17] Carnap [1], pp.7f.

Chapter 2

2.1 The Myths of Consensus and Determinacy

The existence of borderline cases of predicates is made evident in various ways by the linguistic behaviour of speakers: judgements concerning the application of predicates to objects may be inconsistent and there may be uncertainty, manifested in various ways, on the part of users of the language when asked to say whether a predicate applies or fails to apply in certain cases. In section 1.7 we argued that this evidence leads to a certain view of the nature of the borderline case vagueness of natural language. However the usual way in which linguists and philosophers conceive of language seems incompatible with the views of vagueness discussed in the previous chapter. For a natural language, such as English, is usually conceived of as built upon a consensus: words have the meanings and references that they do because of agreement in their application by competent members of the community. Evidence concerning coincidences in the speech behaviour of members of that community supplies the empirical foundation for talk of a communal language and it is usually claimed that those coincidences, or psychological states responsible for them, make it true that a name means one thing rather than another and that a predicate signifies one rather than another determinate set of objects.

Quine's examples of indeterminacy of reference raise doubts about the determinacy thesis.[18] There would seem to be some arbitrariness in deciding upon one semantic account of a natural language when, with a little ingenuity, others may be devised to account for the behavioural evidence equally well. But this criticism does not touch the thesis that natural languages are built upon consensus of the general sort just described.

If, however, there is widespread inconsistency of the kind discussed in the previous chapter and no resolving disputes about the the fringes of a predicate's application then both the consensus and the determinacy would seem to be fictions. Even relative to a set of analytical hypotheses which ascribe a determinate basic ontology to speakers of the language, the behaviour of members of the speech community does not supply grounds for assigning one rather than another determinate set of objects to a vague predicate. And psychological states - intentions and beliefs - which are taken as grounding the representational or classificatory role of uttered expressions are often vague in the sense that it is an indefinite matter which object or set of objects

---

[18] Quine [1], ch.2.

is intended or specified by the utterer. It seems unlikely therefore that this grounding could provide determinate answers in every case to questions about the truth value of meaningful statements of the language.

Despite this, the consensus is often claimed to be genuine. Chomsky argues that its status is that of a necessary idealization of the inconsistency and uncertainty of actual usage.[19] But the necessity for the idealization is grounds for pessimism about the possibility of providing a coherent account of a natural language in which its vagueness is taken seriously. One attempt to deal with the problem is made by Lehrer, who argues in Lehrer [1] that the idea of the consensus may be saved: beneath the uncertainty and inconsistency of idiosyncratic idiolects there is a single precise and determinate language. His argument consists in providing a mathematical model of the consensus. We are to suppose that individuals assign "semantic probabilities" to certain applications of expressions to objects. If the probabilities assigned by all language users were to be surveyed and the information made generally available throughout the community this would have the effect of shifting assignments towards convergence. Some members of the community are likely to be regarded as more authoritative than others on these semantic matters, he says, and so weights might be assigned to each person. Then new, improved semantic measures could be adopted on the basis of weighted averages. Where there is still inconsistency over semantic probabilities new probabilities may be computed on the basis of the information about old assignments. Eventually, Lehrer claims, the process will converge to a limit.

However speakers' uncertainty about the application of predicates to borderline objects might be increased rather than diminished by the results of such a survey. And appeal to linguistic authority is unlikely to be of much help in diminishing doubts unless there is available a theory on which claims to authority can be based. The observational predicates with which we are mainly concerned do not fit into any well developed theory and are applied on the basis of ordinary sense perception. Speakers might well regard their own judgements as being as good as anyone else's on such matters and refuse to budge. Therefore Lehrer's account does not seem to solve the problem of

---

[19] Chomsky [2], pp.188f. and 223f.

reconciling the actual existence of inconsistency with the conception of language as built upon consensus.

2.2 Statistical Regularities and Semantic Determinacy

There may be another reason for the lack of concern about inconsistencies in speech behaviour. This behaviour, which constitutes the only empirical basis for talk of a communal language, might be seen as approximating to a discoverable regular and determinate usage. That is, the fact that that behaviour obeys statistical laws might lead to the hope that actual statistical regularities in usage could be used to settle uncertainties about the limits of application of vague predicates. Resolving this semantic uncertainty could perhaps remove the objections mentioned at the start of this chapter to the use of a formal language as a model of the semantics of a vague natural language. It would also eliminate the dimension of Fregean vagueness concerning boundaries which we have argued to be the source of Sorites problems. So it is worth seeing how such an account of the relation of speech behaviour to vague meanings might be developed.

Black's notion of a consistency profile is intended to provide an account of just this kind.[20] The vague notion of the fringe of application of a word is replaced by precise statistical concepts which allow for quantitative differentiation. The consistency of application of a predicate F to an object b, expressed as C(F,b), is defined as the limit m/n, where m is the number of judgements in a given sample that F applies to b, and n the number of judgements that -F applies to it. A list of exact values of C(F,x) gives an exact description of the vagueness of F. The vaguer the predicate the flatter the curve displayed on the graph corresponding to this linguistic data. The consistency profiles of precise predicates show two horizontal lines joined by a nearly vertical line. The value of C(F,x) for a given object x may be interpreted as the probability of F's application to x. To use F correctly is to use it in conformity with this consistency profile.

One way in which an actual profile for a predicate like "red" might be devised would be by setting up a series of coloured strips, shading gradually from red to orange, and presenting a group of language users with the individual strips in random order, asking each to say whether or not it was red. The group would, of course, have to be a fair sample of language users. Some members might exactly coincide in their use of a particular

---

20 Black [1].

predicate, but not all would: we would expect a range of variation. Some will hesitate over particular strips or may refuse to answer at all. A small amount of vacillation preceding a positive or negative judgement may not matter: deeper uncertainty would have to be ignored since Black's account allows for only positive or negative answers. Methodological decisions will have to be taken to determine which samples are fair ones and how much hesitation time is permitted. One way of solving the latter problem would be to calculate the range of recognition time over the population of the sample for the core cases of things agreed by all to be red and then calculate, for each case of apparent hesitation, the probability that it is just a chance deviation from the norm.

These decisions about sample size and hesitation time will determine a definite profile for each predicate. Though it involves some artificiality and arbitrariness the situation appears at first sight to be no worse than that of many other attempts to abstract some determinate structure from empirical data. The linguistic habits of a population might be represented by more than one such idealization, given different methodological decisions, but the arbitrary choice of any one of these rather than the others will not make much difference, it seems. There are further problems however. The notion of a competent speaker is vague in that there is no sharp division between children and adults: and between subnormal and eccentric users and normal ones. Therefore there can be no sharp divisions between competent and incompetent users of the language and so no sharp boundaries to correct usage. Different decisions on these matters will produce different curves and there does not appear to be any very sharp limits to the range of reasonable decisions which might be made. If this is so the limits to clear and borderline cases of the application of vague terms are hazy - statistical averaging provides no firm answers unless some obviously arbitrary decisions are made.

Context and speaker motivation will also influence the results of the survey by affecting individual decisions about the application of expressions to objects. Mistakes may also be made by competent speakers from time to time. Therefore the limits to the application of the vague predicates should be determined by considering what *most* competent language users would say *most* of the time. If so, they can be drawn only roughly, for "most" is vague in at least two senses. (See 1.3.)

There is also further arbitrariness involved in the selection of the series of colour samples or paradigm objects which is presented to the language users. Obviously the most exhaustive set available with the most gradual variation possible must be chosen. But there are any number of ways of dividing such a series into strips and each alternative slicing of the continuum will produce different answers from language users, different contents for the positive and negative extensions of the predicate and different determinations of truth value for sentences about the colours of objects. The point of introducing this statistical averaging procedure was to abstract one determinate profile of the predicate's application from the inconsistency and indeterminacy of actual usage, but now we find the same inconsistency and indeterminacy infecting the attempt to apply the averaging technique.

There are more serious problems still. If the pattern of use reflected in the profile is to determine further applications of a predicate, all those things which exactly match sample members assigned to a predicate must also be assigned to the same predicate. But there may be further things, outside a given series, which appear to most normal observers to match *both* of a pair of non-matching members of the series, only one of which has been assigned to the predicate. Extrapolating from the responses of observers produces inconsistent results in this situation. Also, no sample series will contain an exhaustive selection of shades of a particular colour, and so some extrapolation based on counterfactual judgements of similarity must be made. These extrapolations could also lead to contradictory assignments by way of further series and Sorites reasoning.[21]

2.3 Vagueness and Convention

The accounts discussed in the last two sections are really attempts to accommodate the evidence for vagueness in the linguistic habits of speakers while treating the language they speak as non-vague. Where vagueness appears in the form of inconsistency and uncertainty it is to be averaged out and so can be ignored. In his book *Convention*, Lewis provides an account of language within which vagueness may be taken more seriously.[22] He also

---

[21] We discuss these issues further throughout part II and especially in chapters 6 and 8.

[22] Lewis does not explicitly mention vagueness in *Convention*. He makes it clear however, in the appendix to "General Semantics" (Lewis [2]) at p.64 that his remarks in Chapter V of *Convention* are intended to provide an account of vagueness in natural language.

provides a sounder foundation for the notion of a communal language than the mathematical consensus or statistical averaging accounts discussed above and supplies an answer to the challenge to clarify the nature of the relation between vague natural languages and their precise formal models.

A language, according to Lewis, is a function L which assigns to every verbal expression Ø in a certain set S an interpretation consisting of a mood m and a truth condition t. S is understood to be the set of sentences of L. t is a set of possible worlds: the worlds in which Ø is true in the case where m is indicative. Further complications are required to accommodate ambiguity, indexicality and anaphora. The two latter phenomena make it better to take the arguments of L to be pairs consisting of a sentence and a possible occasion of its utterance and the existence of ambiguity means that the values of L will be sets of interpretations.

For L to be a possible human language its set of sentences must be finitely specifiable by means of a lexicon containing finitely many constituents as well as a finite set of operations for building complexes from these. Grammars specifying this set also provide interpretations for the lexical items and for sentences built from them by means of projection operations. Names are supplied with interpretations by functions from possible worlds to things in them and n-place predicates receive interpretations by functions from worlds to sets of n-tuples. Ø is true in L on occasion o under interpretation <m,t> iff L assigns to <Ø,o> a set of interpretations containing <m,t> and the possible world w in which o is located is a member of t.

A possible language L is the *actual* language of some population P of speakers when they use L for certain communicative purposes in conformity to convention. Lewis argues in [1] that for the communicative purposes to be served (on the whole) the convention must be one of truthfulness in L. To be truthful in L is to try not to utter any sentence false in L. Only those party to such a convention can use L to acquire and impart information.

Though there is not perfect uniformity in linguistic behaviour there is at least a rough regularity in adhering to a set of restrictions on the production of, and response to, verbal utterances and inscriptions. A regularity R constitutes a convention, in Lewis's sense, when the following conditions obtain:

1) almost everyone conforms to R;
2) almost everyone expects almost everyone else to conform to R;
3) the belief that the others conform to R gives everyone a good and decisive reason for conforming to R;
4) there is a general preference for general conformity to R rather than slightly less than general conformity;
5) where R' is some alternative possible regularity in the behaviour of members of P such that almost no-one could conform to both R' and R, the belief that others conformed to R' rather than R would give everyone a good and decisive reason to conform to R';
6) the facts listed in 1) - 5) are common knowledge among members of P, and it is common knowledge that they are commonly known.

To be a convention a regularity must have a possible alternative: the alternative to truthfulness in L is truthfulness in another language. Since languages are individuated semantically on Lewis's account, alternative languages may have all the same sentences. The identity of a language is determined by its interpretation: no two languages can have the same interpretation. Suppose L and L' are alternative languages which have all the same sentences. They might not generate alternative conventions in the sense required by 5) above since it might be possible to be truthful most of the time in both L and in L'. This could happen where they have overlapping truth conditions. There are, however, plenty of more distant alternatives to each which establish the conventionality of truthfulness in L and in L'. But there may be nothing about the expectations, beliefs, preferences and knowledge of members of P at some particular moment which could decide the question of whether L or L' is their actual language. In other cases inconsistency in speakers' behaviour would sometimes make it clear that they were speaking different precise languages in Lewis's sense.

Lewis accepts this conclusion. He writes:

> A convention of truthfulness in a single possible language is a limiting case - never reached - of something else: a convention of truthfulness in whichever language we choose of a tight cluster of very similar possible languages...Our actual language

> is like a resonance hybrid of the possible languages that make it up. (Lewis [1],p.201.)

This account appears to fit the facts about vagueness discussed in the previous chapter. (Though Lewis is at this point discussing the notion of analyticity it is clear both here and from his later remarks in the appendix to "General Semantics" that he also intends the account to apply to vague natural languages). Lewis points out that inconsistencies between members of the population, and on the part of the same speaker over time do not often hinder communication. Where they do, we simply make temporary conventions which are more restrictive than the permanent ones. He also points out several benefits derived from not restricting ourselves to a single language, the most important of which appears to be flexibility: the adoption of a single precise language might turn out to be inconvenient in the light of new discoveries and theories.

There are two difficulties with this as an account of vagueness in language. Firstly, the speakers of a sharply defined language L are a sub-population of a community of speakers, and which sub-population they are must be unknown to those speakers. Obviously they will not realize that they speak a dialect of English (say) in anything like Lewis's sense: the question is whether their beliefs, expectations and knowledge are really sufficient to give them a good and decisive reason for conforming to the relevant convention. Can it be common knowledge amongst these speakers that conditions 2) to 6) above obtain if they do not know who their co-speakers are, and cannot describe the conventions to which they are supposed to be party?

This objection should not be taken as implying that each individual consistently speaks a single dialect and that the totality of these makes up a cluster of precise languages. Lewis should be understood as claiming that individuals speak a "resonance hybrid" also. The problem remains of how to make sense of the notion of a sharply defined language being one of the actual languages spoken by a certain sub-population when they do not know who their co-speakers are.

Lewis might be taken to be saying either that the rough regularities in behaviour and belief observable in a population P constitutes a family of conventions: conventions of truthfulness in L, truthfulness in L', truthfulness in L" etc.; or, as saying that these rough regularities constitute a single convention of truth in one or other of these precise languages. The difference comes out in the interpretation of 5). On the first view one regularity R might constitute a convention of truthfulness in L and an alternative, R', constitute a convention of truthfulness in a distinct precise language L'. On the second interpretation one rough regularity R constitutes a convention of truthfulness in one or other of the distinct precise languages L, L' etc. and alternatives to R will have to be conventions of truthfulness in other families of precise languages. The second seems a better interpretation, since it allows the regularities to be rough ones. And on p.201 he says:

> The sort of convention I have in mind is this: almost everyone, almost always, is truthful in at least *some* languages of the cluster: but not necessarily the same ones for everyone, or for one person at different times.

On the first interpretation distinct patterns of behaviour would be taken to constitute different conventions of truthfulness in various precise languages. It would not be true that almost all of P conformed to one particular regular pattern or expected everyone else to conform to theirs. On the second, the speakers of a particular precise language do not know who their co-linguists are but this will not matter, for they know (roughly) when others violate the convention to which they adhere. Nor does it matter that they cannot describe the conventions to which they are party so long as they may reasonably be construed as knowing what those conventions are, and as recognizing conformity and non-conformity to them.[23]

The second kind of doubt which might be entertained about this account concerns Lewis's attempt to treat vagueness as a purely pragmatic matter. It is usual to see the vagueness of a language as affecting either its semantics or its logic or both and there appear to be good grounds for this. The possibility of borderline cases of the application of a predicate is often claimed to falsify the semantic principle of Bivalence. And it is argued that the notions of truth and falsehood cannot be the same for vague and for precise languages. Principles of classical logic such as ExM seem threatened also and revision of even such basic rules as Modus Ponens has been suggested as the only means of solving the Sorites Paradox. These are the reasons then

---

[23] See Lewis [3], p.25.

for doubts concerning Lewis's move of deporting vagueness from semantics to the theory of language use.

In the next chapter we shall investigate approaches to vagueness which make it possible to treat languages themselves as vague (rather than just the linguistic habits of a population) and which offer alternative logics and models to the usual ones adequate for precise languages. Lewis seems less than satisfied with his own account in *Convention*: in [2] he suggests an alternative way of treating vagueness within semantics, a suggestion of the general sort we shall investigate in chapter 3. Choosing between these semantic and pragmatic approaches to vagueness depends on how successfully each deals with the problems vagueness presents. We shall postpone a verdict on this until chapter 9. Some of the obscurities in the notion of a "resonance hybrid" may be resolved by considerations we shall introduce there designed to deal with contextual aspects of vagueness.

2.4 Vagueness and Truth Theory

There is another account of natural languages according to which vagueness appears to produce no particular problems or complexities at the level of semantic theory. Some of those who adopt the general approach to the theory of meaning which stems from the work of Davidson have suggested that vagueness presents no special difficulty: a semantic theory for a vague language need not be any more complex than the semantics of a perfectly precise language.

On the Davidsonian approach the task of the semantic theorist is seen as one of outlining the structure of theories of meaning for natural languages and this task is completed once it is shown how to provide a truth theory for those languages of the general form described by Tarski. The claim is, that to specify the meaning of a sentence s of a language L is to lay down necessary and sufficient conditions for the application to s of a predicate which in fact applies to exactly the true sentences of L. For a theory of meaning may be at least expected to provide, for each sentence s of the language, a sentence in a metalanguage specifying the meaning of that sentence. That is, it ought to imply a sentence of the form

M: s means that p

where 'p' is replaced by a sentence which specifies s's meaning. Secondly, it may be expected to do so in a way which shows how the meaning of the sentences depends on their structure and the meanings of their significant parts. For otherwise the theory would make a mystery of our ability to understand on the basis of finite capacities, an infinite number of novel sentences. Thus it must specify the meanings of sentences in such a way as to show how they could be generated out of a finite stock of semantic elements.

Since explanations of meaning may be expected to be of the same uniform kind throughout, it can be argued that an adequate theory must make use of a single key concept in giving the meanings of sentences. Such theories are usually seen as consisting of two parts: a core theory which determines the conditions for the application of the key concept to sentences: and a theory of force, which gives an account of the various kinds of speech act which can be performed by uttering those sentences. There are various arguments for taking truth to be the key concept of the core theory.[24] Since no existing logical apparatus seems adequate to prove sentences containing intensional idioms such as the "means that" in M above, some way must be found of giving the meanings of sentences of the language which does not make use of this construction. And since the resulting theory ought to enable us to make sense of linguistic behaviour, it should furthermore be required to license ascriptions of appropriate propositional attitudes to speakers on the basis of their utterance of various sentences. Thus the sentence p which provides the specification of the meaning of s must specify the content of the propositional act which could be performed by uttering s. Therefore s must (in the indicative case) be a sentence which can be used to assert that p. (The indicative mood is surely primary if we are concerned with the basic function of language as a means of communication). The connexion between truth and assertion is such that any acceptable filling out of the relation between s and p will result in the specification of what are, in fact, truth conditions for s. Therefore truth conditions (appropriately specified) may be used to state the content of assertions.

An adequate theory of truth for a language must be able to generate for each sentence of the language a statement of the truth conditions of that sentence. Homophonic truth theories of the recursive Tarskian variety are one such kind. They are surely adequate since sentences are used to state their own truth

---

24 See, for example, Davidson [1]; McDowell, pp.50f. in Evans and McDowell [1]; and Platts [1], pp.52f.

conditions. The problem of defining the truth predicate is to be solved by constructing a finite set of axioms and rules which imply, for any sentence s which is a member of the set S of sentences of L, a theorem of the form:

s is true iff p.

Tarski claims that a formally correct definition of the symbol 'Tr' for a language L formulated in the metalanguage will be adequate if it is in accord with his convention T:[25]

> CONVENTION T. A formally correct definition of the symbol 'Tr', formulated in the metalanguage, will be called an *adequate definition of truth* if it has the following consequences: (a) all sentences which are obtained from the expression "x $\in$ Tr if and only if p" by substituting for the symbol 'x' a structural-descriptive name of any sentence of the language in question and for the symbol 'p' the expression which forms the translation of this sentence into the metalanguage: (b) the sentence 'for any x, if x $\in$ Tr, then x $\in$ S'...

Where the metalanguage contains the object language 'p' may be replaced by the sentence x itself. Requirements on possible extensional predicates which might be substituted for "means that" turn out to be captured by this criterion also. A suitable predicate will be co-extensive with the truth predicate since an expression may always be correctly used to state its own meaning. These are some of the grounds then, for the claim that it is possible to exploit exactly the same apparatus Tarski uses in his precise account of the way truth conditions of complex sentences are determined by the truth conditions of their components, in order to provide satisfactory theories of meaning for natural languages. So incorporating a recursive definition of truth-in-L is one way of enabling a theory of meaning for L to show how the meanings of sentences are functions of the contained expressions.

It is this special homophonic case which those who claim that vagueness produces no particular problems for semantic theory have in mind. Evans and McDowell in [1] argue that vagueness

---

25 Tarski [1], pp.187f.

in a sentence produces no particular problems for a theory which generates theorems of the form:

s is true iff p,

since vagueness in s is matched by vagueness on the right hand side. The sentence used on the right hand side is either the same sentence or a translation of the one named on the left: in either case vagueness is matched with vagueness. The plausibility of this claim is particularly evident in the former case.

This suggestion only works if the metalanguage of the truth theory is taken to be vague. But then many questions are begged. We cannot take for granted the acceptability of formal theories expressed in a vague language. Grounds will be given in the next chapter for claiming that such languages are inconsistent. We shall see in section 5.6 that a version of the Sorites argument threatens the Evans/McDowell account, since it appears to establish that the existence of vagueness in sentences would import incoherence into the truth theory which made use of them to state their own truth conditions.

There are other more immediate difficulties for the claim that the vagueness of a language has no effect on its semantic theory. The existence of inconsistencies characteristic of a vague language surely ought to complicate the semantic account of such a language. If, as we argued, vagueness surfaces as inconsistency, it appears to threaten the rationale behind accounts of meaning in terms of truth. The rationale was that the truth-theoretic account of the relation between what is said and the world fitted into a wider framework of the explanation of human behaviour. The value of such an account depends upon whether it facilitates general explanations of communication and linguistic understanding. But the existence of inconsistent idiolects surely complicates (or ought to complicate) the picture of assertion and communication of information about the world.

A question which emerges here is whether a homophonic truth-theory for a vague language should be seen as employing a single vague metalanguage, or as ambiguous between a family of precise metalanguages. To see how this is so it is useful to employ a distinction between a syntactic view of truth theories as formal systems consisting of axioms and theorems and the view of them (with which we are usually concerned) as interpreted theories. Talk about truth theories goes on in a meta-meta-language, though we tend to think of this language as identical with the meta-language, particularly when we are considering a truth theory for our own language. However there is a question about the understanding of the meta-language. As a number of writers on truth theory point out,[26] "'Snow is white' is true iff snow is white" expresses no truth to non-English speakers. If vague natural languages are bound to be inconsistent, as we argued above, then the same point may be made about different English speakers, since a number of these might speak what is syntactically the same language but interpret it in different ways. Suppose one person, A, hears another, B, utter the sentence "It is snowing" and suppose further that A knows of no reason to doubt B's veracity and believes B to be in the right causal relation to the weather. A will probably conclude that what B said is true. Using the Tarskian biconditional:

"It is snowing" is true iff it is snowing,

A can arrive at the conclusion that it is snowing. But the first, quoted occurrence of the sentence in the Tarskian truism reports what B said and B may count as cases of snowing, weather conditions A would describe as sleeting rather than snowing. It is not safe therefore for A to conclude that it is snowing. It is not clear what complications ought to be built into truth theory to deal with this difficulty or whether the problem can be met at all. Attempts to fix the interpretation of the meta-language will have to employ some language and the same difficulties will arise again. It is at least clear then, that an account of communication and assertion adequate for vague languages ought to be more complex than one adequate for totally precise languages, in which no doubt or divergence can occur concerning the application of terms to the world.

If languages are individuated *syntactically* it is possible to set up, for any language L, a number of 'truthlike' predicates which meet Tarski's criterion and involve the stipulation of 'satisfactionlike' predicates. The question of which is to be identified with truth in L depends on empirical facts about the use of the language by speakers on various occasions. But if we are considering languages individuated *semantically* each truthlike definition individuates a separate language. The question then arises of which language is the actual language of a given population. But if the arguments of previous sections are correct none of these will coincide with the truth predicate of the language L where L is vague. The arguments mentioned above

---

26 See, for example, Davies [1], p.29.

for the existence of Fregean vagueness can be used to show that no sharply delimited set is determined by actual usage.

Lewis's account at least provides some apparatus for expressing the options. Apart from this, the differences between Lewis's approach and the truth-theoretic one are not great. Although in the model-theoretic possible worlds tradition, Lewis's semantics also make truth a central concept and connect it with a theory of force. The utterance of 'p' by someone endeavouring to conform to a convention of truthfulness will license ascription to them of the belief that p. And much of the Tarskian structure outlined above is reproduced in Lewis's model theory. The difference in which we are interested consists in the cavalier treatment of vagueness in the austere style of truth theory, described above, compared with the account of the relation between the conventions of a vague communal language and the habits of its users provided by Lewis. It remains to be seen in later chapters just how well problems to do with vagueness touched upon here may be dealt with within the framework Lewis provides.

Chapter 3

APPROACHES TO VAGUENESS

In this chapter we shall discuss some of the main approaches to vagueness which have emerged in the literature and use these alternative views to focus on questions to do with the way the semantics and logic of a vague language should be represented. The approaches to be discussed take vagueness seriously, as a phenomenon which is not to be explained away or treated as having no effect on the semantics and logic of a vague language. The questions we shall consider concern the status of the Principle of Bivalence, whether the laws of classical logic hold in a vague language, and the nature of higher order vagueness.

3.1 Borderline Cases, Bivalence and Higher Order Vagueness

On the conception of vagueness which we have been investigating, a predicate is vague when the scope of its application is uncertain, that is, when there are or could be borderline cases of its application. The following three interpretations of the notion of a borderline case may be found in the literature, ours being the third. Taking b to be a borderline case of the predicate F would, on these views, have one or other of the following consequences:

a) b is excluded from the extension of F and from that of non-F,
b) b is partly included in the extension of F and partly excluded from it,
c) it is irremediably uncertain whether b is included in or excluded from the extension of F.

The uncertainty characteristic of vagueness on the third view should be understood to be uncertainty on the part of the theorist over the correct classification of certain items with respect to the predicate F. This uncertainty may be generated by evidence of uncertainty on the part of actual users of the language who hesitate when asked to classify these things, but this is not the only source of doubt. For something may be classified as a borderline case and produce uncertainty on the part of the theorist when it is classified inconsistently, though without apparent hesitation, by all competent users of the language. Since we are considering the question from this point of view we will not discuss the further option:

d) b is both included in and excluded from the extension of F,

for although this reflects the inconsistent applications made by actual language users from time to time it is hard to make sense of it as a distinct option at the level of semantic theory.[27]

We will mainly be concerned in this chapter with the ways in which the first and second views of the nature of borderline cases have been developed, and with investigating their further consequences. It seems that the Principle of Bivalence ought to fail on the first interpretation.

Biv: Every statement is either true or false

must be rejected, since "Fb" will be neither true nor false where b is a borderline case of F-hood. It is not so clear what becomes of this principle on the second and third views. On one interpretation of the second view, "Fb" will be assigned an intermediate truth-value, "I", which is distinct from both "T" and "F". Another obvious way of developing (b), which also rejects Bivalence, would be in terms of a system of continuous degrees of truth: on this view, statements about borderline cases should be assigned one of an infinite range of values between complete truth and complete falsehood. Someone who held interpretation a) might agree with one or other of these views of the status of "Fb", or they might hold that "Fb" lacks a truth-value entirely: where there is vagueness in a language there will be truth-value gaps.

There are alternative ways of understanding c), also. It might be held that this is more adequate than either a) or b) as a statement of what is meant by calling something a borderline case, but that the effect of this uncertainty is again that "Fb" is to be accounted neither true nor false. For the uncertainty is not epistemological: since it can never be resolved by the facts there will never be grounds for assigning either definite truth-value, and if something can never turn out to be true or to be false, it cannot be either. Others might argue that where there is no correct

27 See Thorpe, D. [1] however for an alternative view.

answer to be given to the question of whether "Fb" is true or false, all that can be said is that it is uncertain which it is: we cannot say that it is neither, and so we cannot say (definitely) that Bivalence fails.

So some ways of developing these apparently different views of the nature of borderline cases arrive at the same conclusions about the semantic consequences of supposing a language to be vague. The six alternative views are as follows:

1) "Fb" is neither true nor false; either

   (i) "Fb" is truth-valueless, or

   (ii) "Fb" is to be assigned an intermediate value 'I' distinct from T and from F, or

   (iii) "Fb" is to be assigned some unique value from an infinite range between 0 and 1;

2) "Fb" is either true or false, but it is uncertain which it is, either:

   (i) some presently unknown (but in principle discoverable) facts about the world or our use of language determines which, or

   (ii) some facts about the world or our use of language which are forever hidden from us determine which it is, or

   (iii) the facts fail to determine which it is.

We shall not consider the further possibility, that "Fb" is *both* true and false for the same reason we ignored option d), above. There are, of course, other possible alternatives to 1 (ii) and 1 (iii) but since most accounts of vagueness fall into one or other of the above classes we shall consider just these. It is not clear that there is any very substantial difference between the first two alternatives in 1), that is, between saying there are truth-value gaps and saying there is a third truth-value apart from T and F. Reification of truth-values is no more than a way of trying to make systematic sense of the ordinary use of predicates of truth and falsehood. So it might be argued that there is more of a difference between (ii) and (iii) than there is between (i) and (ii). On the other hand, there is the intuitionist's argument that the supposition that undecidable mathematical statements have a truth-value depends upon unacceptable metaphysics. Their arguments might be taken as providing general grounds for making a distinction between 1) (i) and 1) (ii), for where there are no procedures we can implement which could decide a statement's truth-value, it must be accounted truth-valueless rather than as having a third truth-value.

Assuming then that these are all distinct options, we might go on to ask whether the existence of borderline cases can be blamed on the absence of facts determining a definite truth-value for the statements concerning them, or whether the facts (or lack of them) concerning borderline cases should be taken as establishing that the relevant statements have a truth-value other than T or F (1 or 0). The second does not seem adequate given the conception of vagueness we have been developing. On this conception the borderline status of certain objects is determined by the uncertainty on the part of the theorist over the correct usage of the predicate. But if the facts determine that the borderline case statements have a truth value other than truth or falsehood there need be no such uncertainty: if the facts determine that some statement deserves the value I there is no more room for doubt than there is when other facts determine that other statements are true or are false.

The first, truth-value gap view (1(i)) also seems inadequate given the conception of vagueness we have been developing. The absence of determining facts may sometimes leave observers hesitating over statements containing vague predicates, but in many contexts it seems that there is sufficient ground to assign one or the other definite truth-value to such statements. And often, faced with a borderline case of redness (say) we can see some justification in saying that it is true that it is red, and some, perhaps equally good, justification for saying that it would be false to call it red. No further facts could be imagined (even as available only to an omnipotent being) which could be relevant to the decision on the question, and the facts, such as they are, make it as plausible to apply one as the other. Borderline cases of a predicate are things for which it is rational to apply either the predicate or its negation, it does not seem right therefore to say that the facts determine that vague statements are truth-valueless.

The first two options in the second set seem unsatisfactory also, given the conception of vagueness outlined above. If unknown facts determine whether a statement is true or false it is not vague in the sense which concerns us, and the second kind of view (2 (ii)) raises unanswerable questions about the kind of facts which could decide the issue and why they are forever hidden from us. But it is not clear that the third option (2 (iii)) is a satisfactory one either. If no facts determine whether a statement is true or false how can it be one or the other?

These worries may be spelled out by considering in turn the arguments for and against the view that Bivalence fails because of vagueness. The argument usually given for rejecting Bivalence is that it implies that there must be a definite answer (T or F) to all questions about the truth-value of statements of vague natural languages. But suppose we consider applying the predicate "...is short" to a large number of men arranged in order of height so that the first is clearly very short and the last very tall, but there is no difference detectable without careful measurement between each one and the next? If Bivalence holds, "...is short" must be determinately true or false of each, which means that at some point the predicate suddenly ceases to apply. It is implausible to think there is any such sharp break. Also, to suppose that there is a break somewhere implies that there is a fact of the matter beyond our ken which determines the question one way or the other, and this seems absurd.

However, the rejection of Bivalence in favour of one or other of 1 (i)-(iii) would not seem to solve these difficulties. On the first alternative we say that while some statements predicating shortness of members of the series are true and others false, there is a third class of statements that lack a truth-value. Since there are no further options, there is a last man of whom it can be truly said that he is short, but who differs from the next by some fraction of an inch too small to discriminate with the naked eye. There seem to be no further facts which could determine which man this is. The second alternative has the same problem: there appears to be no advantage to be gained by giving up Bivalence in favour of a principle of Trivalence:

Triv.: Every statement is either T, F or I.

On multivalence accounts there are infinitely many semantic differences all of which are undetectable and there is an arbitrary assignment of one rather than another precise degree of truth to every statement. For nothing about the facts determines that we should assign 0.513 to "Fred is short", rather than 0.512, or 0.5. Even a proponent of a many-valued approach, David Sanford, is forced to admit in [3] (p.201) that "there is something ironic about responding to the imprecision of natural language by adopting a semantics which allows infinitely precise discriminations of truth-value".

So the considerations to do with the vagueness of natural language which were urged against Bivalence seem equally to be problems for the views which reject Bivalence.

A more serious objection to all of the accounts (1(i)-(iii)) is that they fail to reflect the uncertainty which is the essential feature of a vague language. To interpret a) in the first, truth-value gap way is to say that where b is a borderline case of the predicate F, "Fb" has no truth-value. To say this is to dismiss the view that it is true and the view that it is false. The second approach (1(ii)) also provides negative answers to the questions of whether "Fb" is true or whether it is false, questions which were supposed to be undecidable where b is a genuine borderline case. When we declare b a borderline case of F-hood we want to say that it is an uncertain matter whether "Fb" is true or false. To answer these questions in the negative is to ignore doubts about the status of b as possibly within the scope of F. Also, when we say b is a borderline case of F-hood we are declaring it to be an uncertain matter whether "Fb" is true or not. But on all three versions of (1) above "Fb" is not true.[28] It seems then that none of the alternative ways of developing a) or b) suggested above will be adequate as an account of the notion of a borderline case. If borderline cases are genuinely uncertain in this non-epistemic sense, then only the third account, c), will do: lack of certainty concerning the truth-value of a statement is compatible with that statement's being true or being false.

Bivalence does not fail because of vagueness if this is so, for borderline cases provide no counter-examples to it. Counter-examples would have to be statements which are excluded from the scope of truth and falsehood. But this is not implied by the claim that something is a borderline case of a predicate. What we want to say when we declare b a borderline case of F-hood is that it is an uncertain matter whether or not the predicate extends to this object and so whether "Fb" is true or false. If it is an undecidable matter whether or not some statement is true or false, then it is not a counter-example to Bivalence. All we can conclude is that the truth and falsity predicates are vague. This line of

[28] It looks as though the multi-valued account might escape this objection since it can claim to represent b): the view that vague predicates are true of their borderline cases to a degree. So it is not the case that "Fb" is not true, it is just less than completely true. But since "true" is identified with 1 and no statement can be assigned more than one value, the assignment of a degree of truth other than 1 is equivalent to the denial that that statement is true.

argument may lead to the following claim: to pronounce b a borderline case of F-hood is to say that it is *not definitely true that Fb, nor is it definitely false*; to say this is not to say *definitely* that Fb is neither true nor false. does not fail because of vagueness. What does fail is the principle

D.Biv: Every statement is either definitely true or definitely false.

It seems possible to accept Bivalence while rejecting D.Biv There may be thought to be something odd about supposing that a statement which was not definitely true or definitely false was nevertheless either true or false, but this impression can be dispelled by taking the statements in question to vacillate between truth and falsehood. This vacillation corresponds to the inconstancy in actual linguistic usage, which renders the statements undecidable at the theoretical level.

There may be thought to be problems with the claim that Bivalence holds, however. For it may be claimed that to suppose that Bivalence holds would be to suppose that there was a correct answer in every case to the question of whether or not a predicate applied to each object, even though this is at times a genuinely undecidable matter. To suppose this is to collapse 2(iii) into 2(ii). The idea that there is a right and a wrong answer to questions about whether a predicate really applies to one of its borderline cases seems to make the uncertainty epistemic. For it suggests that at least God could tell which truth-value it had, and it is clear that where there is genuine semantic uncertainty no God's-eye view of our language and no uncovering of further facts or extension of our powers could determine which truth-value was correct. But if no information could possibly resolve the question, what point is there to supposing there is a correct and an incorrect answer?

Richmond Campbell argues[29] that we may, nevertheless, retain Bivalence in the face of semantic uncertainty. He points out that there is no contradiction in supposing that a proposition could be true even though there is no possibility, even in principle, of discovering whether or not it is true. He argues that it is compatible with the status of something as a borderline case of a predicate to suppose that there is an unknown correct answer to the question of whether or not that predicate applies to it.

---

29 In Campbell [1], pp.175-191.

The trouble with this view (apart from the obscurity pointed out above) is that it implies that there is a sharp cut-off point in the application of a predicate: for each series of men of increasing height there is an (unknown) last member who is short. And this surely amounts to supposing that there are no borderline cases of "short". There are deeper objections to this view of semantic uncertainty. To suppose that there was some unknown correct answer in every situation to questions about the application of vague predicates would be to go beyond the psychological reality on which language is based. Formal structures which always assigned precise answers could have no claim to be semantics of genuine natural languages.

So there are good reasons against the view that Bivalence holds if it is taken as implying that there is a correct answer to questions about the truth value of all statements. On the other hand, to repeat the claim argued through above, the facts don't appear to make "Fb" anything other than true or false. All the versions of 1) seem unsatisfactory since an adequate supply of facts may leave us uncertain about the truth-value of "Fb": they do not establish that it lacks a truth-value or is something other than true or false. We would be unlikely to treat someone as ill-informed or confused or linguistically incompetent if, in some actual context, they assigned one or other definite truth-value to the predication of "short" of a person we would want to count as a borderline case of shortness. Alternative definite answers are tolerated in such cases, and regarded as appropriate in particular contexts.

The best solution therefore, is to keep Bivalence and argue for c) and 2(iii) as follows. Where F is a vague predicate and b one of its borderline cases, all the facts about b leave it uncertain whether "Fb" is true or false: it is one or the other but they are not sufficient to establish which it is. We must reject the view that Bivalence implies that there is a correct answer to the question of which truth value each statement has. We may in this instance assert a disjunctive statement as true without there being any determinate correct answer to the question of which of its disjuncts are true.

This answer involves steering a line between the extreme realism of those like Campbell, who think reality may render a statement determinately either true or false, even though we could never in principle discover its truth value, and the anti-Realism of those like Dummett, who reject Bivalence on the grounds that the truth or falsehood of statements cannot be independent of our means of recognising the circumstances which justify their assertion or denial.

We shall return to this suggestion in the final chapter. Most of those who have worked on vagueness have argued that Bivalence must be rejected and it is necessary to accept one of the accounts 1 (i)-(iii). Versions of these are investigated in detail in the rest of this chapter. In view of the claims made just above that vagueness of the kind we are interested in is to be identified with non-epistemic uncertainty it may seem hard to motivate an investigation of these alternatives. For none of the versions of (1) can adequately represent this type of uncertainty. It would seem possible, however, to meet some (and perhaps all) of the above objections if an appropriate account of higher-order vagueness could be added to each of 1 (i)-(iii). Consider, for example, the objection to the truth-value gap account: that while it must assume a sharp break between statements which are true and those which lack a truth-value, such breaks are undetectable where we are applying a vague predicate to members of a suitably finely gradated series, and that no extension of our knowledge would help to determine their location. This could be seen as amounting to the claim that the boundaries of the borderline cases are not sharp: there are borderline cases of borderline cases as well as clearly borderline ones. If this is the situation we are in, the "definitely" operator used above to try to justify retaining Bivalence might be useful in giving an account of higher orders of uncertainty concerning the boundaries to the borderline. We could perhaps argue for retaining the principle,

Triv(Gap): Every statement is either true, false or truth-valueless,

in the face of the difficulty of determining which some statements are, so long as we reject

D.Triv(Gap): Every statement is either definitely true, definitely false or definitely truth-valueless

in favour of some more complex set of alternatives. Further borderline cases of these will force a shift to another level, but it seems that at some level the orders of vagueness will run out. Then, it might be argued, a version of 1 (i)-(iii) supplemented by the appropriate account of higher-order vagueness will provide the semantic distinctions required for an adequate account of a vague language. This claim will be investigated further in section 3.4.

3.2 Bivalence and Excluded Middle

It is sometimes claimed that arguments against Bivalence apply also to the Law of Excluded Middle. If the existence of borderline cases of the application of a predicate renders some statements neither true nor false then it would seem that

ExM: For any statement P, either P or not-P

is not a law. For suppose P lacks a truth value, then not-P is truth-valueless also and neither disjunct is true. Where P fails to be either true or false, neither disjunct can be true. If P is not true the first disjunct cannot be true and, if P is not false either, not-P cannot be true. Then neither arm of the disjunction could be true. It is argued that a disjunction is only true when one or other of the disjuncts is true. If so, then borderline cases interpreted in the first way would seem to provide counter-examples to ExM.

However it is not immediately clear that the disjunction fails to be true where this is accepted, for it is not clear what effect indefiniteness of constituents has upon the truth-value of the complex sentences in which they occur. The introduction of "I", for example, must affect the meaning of the connectives which were defined in terms of truth tables with only two values. It can also be argued that the introduction of "I" affects the meaning of "true" and "false". So a negative answer to the question of whether every sentence is either true or false does not determine whether (P v -P) ought to be accounted a theorem of any logic adequate to represent the workings of a vague language.

It is often claimed that ExM implies Bivalence, and so if Bivalence is rejected ExM goes too. But the implication from the claim that (P v -P) is a theorem of a system to the claim that each wff in a system is either true or false depends upon the meaning of "true" expressed in Tarski's criterion T:

Tr(P) iff P

(or at least one half of it). Unless it is possible to get from P and from -P as assumptions to (Tr(P) v Tr(-P)), Bivalence cannot be proved. But where P is assigned I, criterion T seems dubious. For 'I' was introduced in the last section as meaning neither true nor false, and so the biconditional (Tr(P) iff P) cannot be valid. Where P is neither true nor false the claim 'P is true' would seem to be false. At best the consequent of (P $\rightarrow$ Tr(P)) will be I, since the antecedent is I and the consequent either F or I. Either way it will not be assigned T in this case.

It might be thought that though Bivalence is rejected by the three accounts 1) (i)-(iii) discussed in the last section, each of them is committed to the following weakened version of Bivalence,

W.Biv: (Tr(P) v -Tr(P))

from which ExM follows. (-Tr(P) is to be understood here as encompassing two possibilities: P false, and P indefinite.) But although the converse implication, from ExM to W.Biv, seems very plausible (since W.Biv looks like no more than a substitution instance of ExM), the implication in the other direction, from the assumption of W.Biv to the truth of ExM, does not hold. For although (Tr(P) v -Tr(P)) is true where P is assigned I, it is hard to justify assigning (P v -P) anything better than I in this circumstance. It would be possible to derive ExM from W.Biv using Vel. introduction and elimination rules if we could help ourselves to

$$-Tr(P) \rightarrow Tr(-P)$$

as well as criterion T, but neither seems acceptable. The former cannot be right since from it and the clearly correct

$$Tr(-P) \rightarrow False(P),$$

it would follow by transitivity that

$$-Tr(P) \rightarrow False(P)$$

which we obviously don't want to accept. ((Tr(-P) → False(P)) has to be correct since Tr(-P) rules out the possibilities that Tr(P) and Indefinite(P). The latter would make -P indefinite also. So all that is left is False(P).) Tarski's T seems doubtful here for reasons similar to those outlined in the last paragraph.

So when "not true" no longer means just "false", it is not at all clear whether or not ExM ought to be considered a law. The arguments above depend on certain assumptions about the meanings of the connectives in this situation and, as mentioned before, it is not clear what effect the introduction of alternatives to truth and falsehood will have on the meanings of connectives defined in terms of the standard truth tables. Perhaps the most straightforward, plausible account of the consequences of introducing "I" are given by Kleene's strong tables:[30]

---

30 Kleene [1], pp.334f.

-P		P&Q				PVQ				P→Q				P≡Q			
P	-P	P\Q	T	F	I	P\Q	T	F	I	P\Q	T	F	I	P\Q	T	F	I
T	F	T	T	F	I	T	T	T	T	T	T	F	I	T	T	F	I
F	T	F	F	F	F	F	T	F	I	F	T	T	T	F	F	T	I
I	I	I	I	F	I	I	T	I	I	I	T	I	I	I	I	I	I

Kleene argues that this system involves the least possible departure from classical logic in the sense that truth-values of complex sentences governed by logical constants are determined in a systematic truth-functional way. Also the tables are *regular* in the sense he defines, and this appears to be an important advantage over non-regular tables. A table is regular in this sense iff it assigns T (or F) at an "I" row (or column) only if the row (or column) contains all Ts (or all Fs). As a result of this feature, any compound which would be assigned a definite truth-value on the standard tables will be assigned that same definite truth-value by these tables. This is surely correct where I is assigned to a sentence because of vagueness: this assignment ought not to have the effect of making complexes containing the sentence indefinite where the conditions for the assignment of truth or falsehood on the standard tables are already met. A decision one way or the other on the indefinite constituent should not make any difference to the truth-value of the whole. A disjunction with an indefinite disjunct ought to count as true when the other disjunct is true, for there is no way it could turn out to be false.

To give substance to this notion of deciding one way or other on an indefinite constituent it is not necessary to suppose that, at some mythical future stage in the development of the language, the meanings of the words contained in the sentence might be refined in such a way that the sentence comes to be accounted either true or false. It is only necessary to imagine that circumstances arise in which it is necessary in some context to lay down stipulations sufficient to determine the truth-value of the constituent in that and similar contexts. We saw earlier that it does not conflict with the meaning of vague expressions to treat them in this way in particular contexts.

On Kleene's account, ExM turns out not to be a law since a disjunction with indefinite disjuncts will be indefinite. However, on the rationale for accepting these regular tables it seems that it ought to hold: where both disjuncts are assigned "I" there is no way the disjunction (P v -P) could turn out false.

(P → P) and (P → --P) fail as well though, intuitively, there appears to be no reason why the presence of vagueness should have this effect. It turns out that none of the laws of classical logic holds in Kleene's system, and in this sense it involves a large departure from classical logic.

Whether or not there is taken to be a connexion in either direction between ExM and Bivalence depends on what other assumptions are made and on the kind of logical system adopted. It is possible to reject ExM and keep Bivalence. Kleene appears to take this line, since his 'I' ('U' in his notation) means "true or false but undecidable at present which". (The uncertainty here is clearly intended to be epistemic, not semantic.) It is also possible to reject Bivalence and keep ExM. In section 3.4 we shall discuss a non-truth-functional account which adopts this alternative.

3.3 Vagueness and Logic

It might be argued that to understand the connexion between vagueness and uncertainty we must accept the need for a scale of degrees of truth and falsehood corresponding to the amount of uncertainty which exists concerning the application of the predicate to various borderline objects. The claim is that where predicates are vague, it cannot be assumed that things are contained in their extensions in the way in which things are normally contained in sets. Vague predicates require the notion of a fuzzy set, things are contained within it to a degree. The degrees of truth and falsehood which vague statements may have are represented by the closed interval (O,1). Predicates are functions from sets of individuals onto (O,1), the continuity of the set of possible values reflecting the range of applicability of the predicate to possible borderline cases. Since there may be a continuum of such cases we need the unit interval, with O representing complete falsehood and 1 complete truth. A systematic account of this interpretation of the notion of a borderline case may be given provided that where n is the degree to which a vague statement Fb is true, the value of -Fb is (1-n). There are various systems of fuzzy logic which meet this constraint.

Machina, in [1] and [2], adopts Lukasiewicz's system Lx. Taking "/" to mean "the value of", the following truth conditions hold.

1) $/-P/ = 1 - /P/$

2) $/P \& Q/ = \text{Min}(/P/,/Q/)$

3) $/P \vee Q/ = \text{Max}(/P/,/Q/)$

4) $/P \rightarrow Q/ = 1$ where $/Q/ > /P/$; or $= 1 -/P/ +/Q/$ where $/P/\geq/Q/$

5) $/(\forall x)A(x)/$ = the greatest lower bound of the values $/A(t)/$ for each name t

6) $/(\exists x)A(x)/$ = the least upper bound of the values $/A(t)/$ for each name t.

As a consequence of 2) conjunctions of the form (P & -P) may be partially true. To some this has seemed sufficient ground for rejection of this view.[31] ExM fails as well as the Law of Non-Contradiction. For by 3), when P is less than completely true (P v -P) will fail to be completely true also. The logic preserves truth-functionality but at the cost of losing laws of logic. Machina tries in [2] to justify this consequence, claiming that vagueness makes it reasonable to both assert and deny a statement. But since an assertion can only be an assertion of truth and a denial of a statement a denial of its truth, the claim that it may be reasonable to do both would seem to severely restrict our scope for ever being unreasonable.

Alternatively, we would have to divorce truth from the notion of assertion, so that to assert a statement is not to assert its truth. But it is difficult to see how the notion of truth could be divorced from the notion of assertion.

Should vagueness affect logic? The use of classical principles in Sorites arguments involving vague terms is claimed to lead to contradictions. We shall examine these claims closely in Part II and shall argue finally that the problem can be solved without giving up those principles. Apart from the Sorites, the presence of vagueness in language does not seem to provide good reason for thinking that laws of classical logic do not apply. We saw above that the mere existence of borderline cases does not seem to force revision of these principles - at least this is so if borderline cases merely introduce uncertainty concerning the

[31] See Kamp [1].

application of the predicate. Another reason often cited for the claim that vagueness requires a special non-classical logic is the inconsistency evident in natural languages and it is of course this that Machina is appealing to in claiming that it may be reasonable to assert contradictions. The inconsistencies in the use of vague predicates noted in chapter 2 stop short of outright contradictions, however. Speakers' assignments of predicates to the same objects within a context may conflict, and a single speaker may make inconsistent applications of a predicate over time and in different contexts. The vagueness of many predicates may make these conflicting assignments reasonable ones to make in various contexts, but it is hard to see how it could make the assertion of a contradiction on the part of a single speaker in some context reasonable. Nevertheless, where F is a vague predicate and b one of its borderline cases, competent users of the language are sometimes willing to assent to the claim that b is both F and non-F. The conclusion often drawn from this is that vague languages are either incoherent or require a non-standard logic in which contradictions are permissible to a degree.

If these were the only options the second would seem the better. But vagueness may be seen as involving context-dependence and, when it is, reasonable interpretations can be found for these apparent contradictions. "b is F and b is non-F" may be understood as a true claim that each conjunct has an appropriate and reasonable application in a distinct context, relative to a speaker. Observational predicates are meant to be applied to objects on the spot without careful calculation or checking of the record of past reports, and so individuals will inevitably be inconsistent from time to time in their application of such predicates, and will differ from one another in their judgement concerning the applicability of such predicates to particular objects. Inconsistency is tolerated, and there is not even any sense of real conflict. Discrepant judgements within a certain range are all regarded as perfectly reasonable, no-one being in a position to correct others' conflicting predications or to retract their own previous ones as mistaken. So the statement "b is F and non-F" is better seen as a recognition of this scope for alternative classificatory decisions in different contexts, than as an abandonment of the Law of Non-Contradiction. We shall spell out this suggestion in sections 9.9 and 9.10.

Comparison with other sorts of cases where revision of logic has been suggested provides further grounds for holding that vagueness is compatible with classical logic. Ordinary borderline cases are not the kind of thing one tries to imagine when considering whether -(P & -P) could ever fail, or whether there could possibly be counter-examples to (P v -P). The discoveries of quantum mechanics may make these possibilities worth taking seriously. But merely pointing out a borderline case of redness (or of some other vague predicate) does not seem to provide a clear counter-example to these principles.

Perhaps the strongest argument for the claim that the logic of vagueness must be non-classical is the claim that vague predicates are predicates of degree. If natural language predicates apply to things in the world to varying degrees, statements in those languages may be true to varying degrees. The assignment of 0.5 to statements is not compatible with the Principles of Excluded Middle or Non-Contradiction. (At least this is so given any reasonable interpretation of negation.) As noted in section 1.7, the existence of continua in nature makes it plausible to suppose that many natural language predicates apply to things in the world with varying degrees of justice. This is the most plausible motivation then for the systems of logic based on the assignment of degrees of truth to statements.

One difficulty with the idea that a systematic account of borderline case vagueness must allow for continuous degrees of truth is that there is not always a natural ordering of the borderline cases of a predicate with respect to the degree to which it applies to them. The situation is at least complicated by the existence of multi-dimensionally vague predicates such as "clever". It might be possible to find a number of criteria determining scales by which more or less clever people could be compared, but this seems dubious. Another problem concerns the grounds for assigning one rather than another precise degree of truth to a vague statement. Both questions are discussed by Machina in [1] and [2]. He claims there that empirical investigation would reveal a natural ordering and non-arbitrary measure of degrees of confidence of language users in different propositions. For reasons which have already been discussed in section 2.2 this does not seem satisfactory.

In many cases it seems that the applicability of a predicate for an individual language user is determined by some idiosyncratic weighting of the members of a characteristic package of properties. The results of a single individual's weightings will vary from context to context and there will also be variation from one language user to another, but provided the alternatives are within some roughly specifiable range they will be regarded by the community as acceptable. In other cases generally accepted criteria for the application of a predicate conflict or, alternatively, simply fail to determine whether or not some object is to be included within the extension of the predicate. Again, any decision made in a specific context by an individual language user is deemed acceptable if it is within a roughly specifiable range.

Machina does attempt to build sufficient complexity into his account to accommodate these contextual features. In the first sort of case of weighting vagueness he allows that some members of the domain may be in the extension of the predicate only to a limited extent. Where it is an undecidable matter whether or not some object b within the domain of discourse is within the fuzzy extension of the predicate, the statement "Fb" is to be assigned 0.5. In other cases where there is conflict between the semantic rules or criteria determining the application of a predicate, he decrees that a predicate letter should be assigned more than one fuzzy partial extension. Each is supposed to correspond to the extension fixed by one consistent set of criteria. The valuation of statements containing the predicate is settled by taking an appropriately weighted average of the values obtained for each set of criteria. This is spelled out in the conditions which he says the valuation function of an interpretation for a vague language must meet. The relevant clauses specify that

(i) D is a non-empty set, called the domain of the interpretation;

(ii) and I a set, called the index of the interpretation containing at least three elements: "In","Out" and "Borderline";

(iii) and E is a set of possible extensions consisting of all the ordered pairs whose first members are n-place predicate letters ($n \geq 1$) and whose second members are ordered n-tuples of elements of D, the number of places of the predicate letter equalling the number of places in the n-tuple;

(iv) F is a finite set of predicate interpretation functions, each of which has a subset of E as its domain and a subset of I as its range;

(v) d a denotation function which assigns to each individual constant an element of D and an individual constant to each element;

(vi) and v a valuation function which assigns to each sentence letter and to each n-place predicate letter followed by n terms a value in [0,1], to variables, members of D, and to wffs assignments matching conditions 1) - 6) above. The assignment made by v to an n-place predicate letter followed by individual constants $<a_1,.....,a_n>$ depends on the value assigned to $f(<\phi,<a_1,...,a_n>>)$.[32]

Furthermore, Machina lays down that

(vi.1) If only one element, f, of F interprets ϕ at $<a_1,..a_n>$, then $v(\phi(a_1,..a_n)) = f(<\phi<a_1,...a_n>)$.

(vi.2) If no elements of F interpret ϕ at $<a_1,...a_n>$, then $v(\phi(a_1,..a_n)) = .5$.

(vi.3) If more than one element of F interprets ϕ at $<a_1,..a_n>$, then "$v(\phi(a_1,...a_n))$ shall be chosen so as to lie somewhere within the range of values given to $<\phi,<a_1,...,a_n>>$ by these elements of F.[33]

These adjustments to the theory are artificial and arbitrary in various ways. Different appropriate weighted averages could be found which conflicted in their assignment to particular statements. The conflict is between vague, not precise, criteria. And where it is a genuinely undecidable matter whether or not some object is within the extension of a predicate the question ought not to be definitely resolved by an account which is intended to respect vagueness. As we saw in earlier sections, vagueness surfaces in natural languages as inconsistency: the application of vague predicates to objects may vary from speaker to speaker, and on the part of the same speaker from time to time and context to context. So a sentence containing a vague predicate may get the whole range of semantic assignments from wholly true to wholly false.Consequently, an assignment of a value other than 0 or 1 to a statement would in many cases be at odds with any decision actually made by an individual language user or community when they eventually considered what should be said about a borderline case of some vague predicate. In a legal

32 We spell out details of this dependence later.

33 Machina [2], p.68.

context for example, where it must be decided whether or not a tricycle is a vehicle, the valuation will be either 0 or 1, never 0.5. Where we don't have to decide such questions there seems to be no substantial reason for assigning one rather than another degree of truth. There is just no truth of the matter as to which is correct.Any model intended to reflect and explain the vagueness of natural languages could not adequately do so if it eliminated this diversity by averaging out alternative linguistic responses to borderline cases. For it could equally well serve as a model of a precise language.

We saw in chapter 1 that it is essential to the vagueness of natural language predicates that there be a range of acceptable but inconsistent answers to questions about the applicability of a vague predicate to its borderline cases. But if this is so, then given any assignment of a determinate degree of truth > O and < 1 to an atomic sentence, it is possible to find another assignment which is just as good, that is, which may be argued to be just as appropriate (on some reasonable construal of the data) to the linguistic dispositions of the population which speaks the language (see section 2.2). One thing which distinguishes borderline cases is the uncertainty which attaches to assignment of truth values to statements involving them.

Since many of the problems raised in the last few paragraphs have already been discussed in chapter 2, we shall not pursue them further here. A proponent of fuzzy logic might always respond to our arguments by claiming that the assignment of degrees of truth to statements is no more than a formal device designed to illustrate the way the logic and semantics of a vague language works. Arbitrary assignments are justified so long as they provide a suitable spread of values. This reply might be acceptable if the challenge outlined at the beginning of chapter 2 could be met: the challenge to provide a precise account of natural language which does not simply eliminate its vagueness. We have found evidence so far that the vagueness of natural language is Fregean (section 1.7) and it does appear that fuzzy logic fails to accommodate vagueness of this strong variety. For it is supposed that there are sharp limits to the range of the borderline cases of a natural language predicate, a definite point where it ceases to be completely true that the predicate applies to some object and begins to be slightly less than true.

At this point it seems that an account of higher-order vagueness might enable the proponent of fuzzy logic to resolve the problem. As well as providing the means to accommodate this last difficulty about borderline cases of borderline cases, it would seem to supply answers to earlier questions concerning the compatibility of this account with the uncertainty we are claiming to be characteristic of vagueness. We shall investigate the prospects for supplementing fuzzy logic accounts with systems of higher order vagueness in section 3.5.

3.4 Supervaluations

The claim that the limits of application of certain predicates of natural language is unclear is often interpreted to mean that there is a range of distinct, acceptable ways of drawing boundaries to their scope. These could be regarded as alternative ways of precisifying those predicates. On this view, an object b counts as a borderline case of a predicate F when there are acceptable ways of precisifying the meaning of the predicate which would result in the object's falling within its scope, and other, perhaps equally good ways of precisifying its meaning which would result in the exclusion of that object.

This interpretation of vagueness is developed by Kit Fine in "Vagueness, Truth and Logic".[34] For each vague predicate of the language there is a class of precisifications whose members are determined by the vague meaning of the predicate. Vagueness is underdetermination of meaning, a source of truth value gaps which could only be closed if the language were to become precise. The possibilities for making a predicate precise are delimited, according to Fine, by its potential meaning. He writes:

> In understanding a language one has thereby understood how it can be made more precise; one has understood ... the possibilities for its growth. (Fine [1], p.277.)

As mentioned earlier, Fine believes all vagueness in language to be reducible to vagueness in predicates. A statement is vague just when it contains vague constituents. A vague statement is true, according to Fine, just when it is supertrue: true for all ways of making its vague constituents perfectly precise.

(a) Specification Spaces

A proper account of the semantics of a vague language requires, Fine claims, the notion of *specification space* containing a

---

34 Fine [1].

number of points, each specifying an interpretation for a language. A *partial specification* is an assignment of one or other of the values T, F or I to each of the atomic statements of the language. A space is said to be *admissible* if it is in accord with the intuitively understood meanings of the predicates. So "I" is assigned only to sentences of the language which some speakers would take to be uncertain in truth value.

Points in a space are ordered by an *extension* relation which preserves definite truth and falsehood: t extends u (t>/u) iff t assigns definite truth wherever u does. A *resolution condition* determines that a statement assigned I at some point u will be resolved in each way (as true and as false) at distinct points which extend u. Intuitively, each extension can be seen as a stage in the possible precisification of the language. Spaces may be required to have a *base point*: the point which all other specifications extend. Fine puts a further requirement of *completeability* on spaces. This is the requirement that every point in a space can be extended to a complete point, complete points being ones which assign only the definite truth-values T and F.

Spaces containing only admissible specifications are deemed *appropriate*, and truth-valuation is based upon an appropriate space. Possible truth conditions must meet two constraints: the *stability* condition requires that any statement assigned a definite truth-value at some point has the same definite truth-value at all extensions of that point, and the *fidelity* condition ensures that a statement is true (or false) for a complete specification iff it is classically true (or false). A statement assigned different definite truth-values at different points is neither true nor false in that space: it is said to be supertrue iff it is true in all admissible and complete specifications in the space; it is superfalse iff it is false at all such admissible and complete specifications.

There are further restrictions on the assignment of truth-values to complex wffs due to a phenomenon Fine calls "penumbral connexion". He claims that the existence of such connexions makes all truth-functional accounts unsatisfactory. Penumbral connexions are meaning relations and may be of two sorts. External penumbral connexions hold between different predicates when precisifying one fixes the scope of the other. So where, for example, the predicate "red" is to be precisified by determining which wavelengths of reflected light are to count as within its scope, particular decisions will also help to determine which things count as orange, and as pink etc. Internal penumbral connexions determine systematic treatment of different borderline cases of the same predicate. So the decision to call Roger bald when he has some number n of hairs must, on any systematic account which respects penumbral connexions, fix what can be said concerning the baldness of other borderline cases with fewer than n hairs.

(b) External Penumbral Connexions and Uncertainty Fine claims that the assignment of truth values to vague complex sentences depends on our conception of ways of making precise the predicates contained in the component sentences. Since any sharpening up of the predicate "pink" will affect the boundaries of the predicate "red", the complex sentence "b is pink and b is red" will be false, even where b is an object intermediate in shade between the two. In this case the component statements are neither true nor false. If these external penumbral connexions exist, any truth-functional account of the logic of a vague language (such as Kleene's three-valued one or the fuzzy logics discussed above) must be rejected. Suppose R stands for the statement "b is red" and P for the statement "b is pink", and b is a borderline shade between these two colours. According to Fine (P v P) should count as indefinite, as it does in Kleene's tables, but (P v R) is true, since any sharpening which makes one contained statement false will make the other true. (It is assumed that pink and red are the only options, nothing could be a borderline case of a third shade also.) Since in both cases ((P v P) and (P v R)) the disjuncts were assigned "I", no truth-functional account will be able to assign correct truth conditions. Similarly, (P & R) is false since precisifying cannot, Fine claims, make b a case of both redness and pinkness, though on truth-functional accounts such as Kleene's it is indeterminate. But where S stands for the statement "b is round" and b is also a borderline case of roundness, (P & S) is indefinite. Statements of the form (P & -P) are always false, according to Fine, whether or not P is indeterminate, for any sharpening which makes P true will make -P false, and vice versa. And though P and R are both indeterminate, (P $\rightarrow$ -P) is not true, whereas (P $\rightarrow$ -R) is true.

Truth conditions for a vague language are stated using the extension relation and taking t to be an admissible specification point. The truth conditions he formulates seem to be in line with the rationale Kleene advanced in favour of his strong tables. For the they ensure that I is assigned to complexes only when precisification of constituents would fail to determine truth-value. Where alternative ways of rendering constituents precise would have the same effect on the truth-value of the whole, there is no reason to regard that complex as less than definite in truth-value.

A formula A is *valid* according to Fine iff it is true in all specification spaces.[35] B is a consequence of A if, for any specification space, B is true whenever A is.

Two questions must be considered concerning Fine's arguments against truth-functionality. It is not immediately obvious why the assignment of truth-values to complex sentences should be made to depend on our conception of ways of making their constituents precise. Why should the assignment of truth value to a vague sentence of this language depend on what *would* be assigned to the sentence in various possible, totally precise, non-existent languages? Acceptance of this rests on adopting Fine's view of vagueness as similar to ambiguity: a vague statement glosses alternative precise meanings. If this view of vagueness is accepted, then it is surely right to base a logic and truth conditions for a vague language on the various resolutions of the vague statement and their relations with one another. To accept this view of vagueness is to endorse the second interpretation of the weak borderline case conception discussed in chapter 1: it is to see a borderline case as a potential member of the extension of the predicate.

The second question to be considered concerns the limitations Fine places on acceptable ways of precisifying vague predicates. It is sometimes objected that his arguments against truth-functionality do not accord with intuitions about the truth-values of complex statements containing indeterminate components. The statements (P & R) and (P v R) are considered by some to be indeterminate in truth value, rather than false and true respectively as Fine thinks. As we saw in the last section, Machina claims that it is natural to take (P & -P) to be at least partly true where P is indeterminate in truth-value, and he also claims that (P v -P) is less than completely true where P stands for a sentence containing a vague predicate.

Despite these intuitions, shared by some but not all writers on the subject, it seems plausible to suppose, with Fine, that there are some penumbral connexions between predicates. On the view

---

35 It is necessary to include spaces in which penumbral connexions are not respected otherwise truths based upon them would have the status of laws of logic.

of vagueness as akin to ambiguity, any systematic assignment of truth-values seems to require that if P is assigned true at some point it cannot also be assigned false at that point. For that reason it seems that (P & -P) should be assigned superfalse in appropriate spaces, and (P v -P) and (P → P) assigned supertrue. Any determination of the limits of application of "pink" will surely affect the scope of its negation in any coherent system of precisification. What is not obvious however, is how it will affect the scope of *other* predicates to which it is penumbrally related.

Penumbral connexions may be looser than Fine thinks for there seem to be ways of achieving overall consistency which he does not consider. It does not seem incompatible with the vague meanings of "pink" and "red" to suppose that some precisifications of their regions of application allow for overlap. It seems that such sharpenings must be consistent with some potential for refining the meanings of the predicates, since competent users of the language do not universally reject (P & R) and many hesitate over (P → -R) when confronted with borderline cases. But these intuitions might all be accepted without affecting the arguments concerning the laws of logic for they concern only non-logical relations between different predicates.

Systematic treatment of precisifications seems to force acceptance of the laws of logic but not the definite and restricted meaning connexions between predicates which Fine claims to hold. External penumbral connexions exist, but they seem to be looser and vaguer than he allows for. But if it is a vague matter whether or not some penumbral connexions obtain, then it becomes uncertain what truth value should be assigned to certain non-atomic statements. The obvious move would be to try to incorporate both lax and strict policies in precisifying vague predicates by generalizing over specification spaces. While (P & R) is superfalse in spaces in which no precisifications of penumbrally connected predicates allow for overlap, it is indeterminate in spaces which allow as admissible points at which overlap of predicates is permitted and the conjunction is thereby assigned true. But generalizing over these kinds of spaces would amount to accepting the slack policy. It would not give us what is wanted: a reflection of the uncertainty which attaches to the question of which policy is right. The vague meanings of natural language predicates do not provide clear limits to the acceptable ways of precisifying them.

(c) Internal Penumbral Connexions and the Sorites
Provided Fine's general account of vagueness is accepted the existence of at least some penumbral connexions vindicates Fine's attitude to classical logic and the truth conditions he specifies. Fine claims that this account provides a solution to the Sorites paradox: it turns out, he says, that one premiss of the reasoning fails. It is superfalse that for any number n,

> If a man with n hairs on his head is bald, then a man with (n+1) hairs is bald also,

for each extension of a specification point in an appropriate space has some complete and admissible extension which assigns false to the conditional contained within the scope of the quantifier. Different extensions may make the break at different places since they correspond to different possible precisifications of the predicate "bald", but since all will have a sharp cut-off point in terms of numbers of hairs, the general conditional will be false at all points.

There is a rather general difficulty with the suggested approach to the Sorites: a problem which casts doubt on Fine's conception of vagueness. Internal penumbral connexions concern relations between borderline cases of the same predicate. The meanings of those predicates are supposed to determine that if one man is bald and a second has less hair than the first, the second is bald also. Consistency clearly requires that this connexion hold. But these meanings on which the penumbral connexions depend are not precise: small differences don't affect the application of the predicate. If internal penumbral connexions stretch in the other direction also we may have to accept

> If one man is bald and a second has just one more hair, then the second is bald also.

Fine says nothing about internal penumbral connexions which excludes this conclusion, and what he does say supports it. For penumbral connexions are supposed to depend on meaning relations, and intuitions about the meaning of "bald" support this conditional. The meaning of "bald" is such that one hair either way is not sufficient to make a difference to the applicability of the predicate. But this is, of course, an argument against the whole precisification approach. If it is accepted, there can be no systematic treatment of truth conditions by way of precisifications, for there can be no sharp divisions of the required sort.

This problem is closely connected with another. The semantics for Fine's supervaluation system require the notion of an appropriate space: the space which, for a given language, contains all the admissible specifications of truth-values for atomic sentences of that language. But it seems unlikely that the vague meanings of the predicates of natural language could determine sharp upper or lower bounds to the set of admissible precisifications. If they did, there would be sharp limits to the class of borderline cases of each predicate. The same problem which led to the provision of a range of specifications rather than just one interpretation for the language now makes the sharp boundaries of the range of admissible specifications seem arbitrary. Given any decision about the limits of this range, it is surely possible to argue that just one more (or just one less) specification should be counted as admissible. We shall see in the next section whether this latter problem may be overcome by a satisfactory account of higher order vagueness.

3.5 Approaches to Higher Order Vagueness

We have argued above that there is a kind of uncertainty and indefiniteness of a semantic variety which is characteristic of vagueness and which cannot be reflected in the models for vague languages offered by systems of fuzzy logic or supervaluation semantics. The former assign precise degrees of truth to vague statements and sharp limits to the class of borderline cases of a vague predicate. Supervaluation accounts also imply that there are sharp limits to the boundaries of the borderline cases because limits are drawn to the ways of making vague predicates precise. But if language is vague in Frege's sense there are no sharp boundaries to the application of vague predicates. A natural response is to say that the uncertainty characteristic of vagueness merely concerns which degrees of truth are to be assigned to a given statement, or which set of sharp boundaries to the borderline best represent the vagueness of the language, and that an account of higher order vagueness will resolve the difficulty. We shall argue in the next two subsections that this solution fails.

(a) Fuzzy Logics and Higher Order Vagueness

On the fuzzy logic account the hazy boundaries to the range of borderline cases would have to be represented by subtle variations in the degrees of truth awarded to different statements which fall short of full truth and falsehood. But to assign precise degrees of truth is to assume that there is a sharp division between statements which are completely true and those which are slightly less than true and so to assume that there are sharply defined limits to the borderline cases of vague predicates. At least this seems to be a consequence of the view of matters put forward by Goguen who takes semantic models to be "purely exact constructions" (Goguen [1], p.327). No assertions of truth to a degree can be uncertain. Machina's views about the possibility of vagueness and uncertainty in the semantic metalanguage are less clear. He admits that assignments of degrees of truth to statements of a vague language will be underdetermined by the empirical data about the use of the language, but thinks we should accept a degree of arbitrariness here.

This issue revives doubts about the artificiality of the determinacy of assignments of degrees of truth in fuzzy logic accounts. The worry can be given more force now for it appears that the fuzzy logic account really involves treating language as if it were only first order vague, and as we have seen there are good reasons for thinking it contains predicates which have a higher order of vagueness. To assign determinate degrees of partial truth in all cases eliminates a dimension of vagueness in natural language, for it amounts to ignoring the uncertainty which infects the ascription of truth to many statements. We argued earlier on that this uncertainty is a mark of vagueness.

It might be thought that despite Goguen's view about the determinacy of assignments of degrees of truth and the tendency on the part of most exponents of fuzzy logic to ignore higher orders of vagueness it might be possible to give some account of levels of vagueness within the fuzzy logic account. It turns out, however, that it is hard to make sense of the idea that assignments of truth-values to sentences could be less than perfectly determinate. Bertil Rolf argues in Rolf [1] that it cannot be done for the following reason. Suppose the valuation function V assigns 0.68 to the sentence "It is raining at time t in Melbourne". (We will call this sentence S.) Could the sentence "S is true to degree 0.68" be less than completely true? Let us suppose now that it could, and that it is to be assigned 0.92. Then perhaps the sentence "S is true to degree 0.7" might be truer - maybe this sentence gets 0.98. This is all extremely artificial; we saw earlier that actual language use is not precise and definite enough to justify such claims. But now there is a more serious problem. For it surely makes no sense to suppose that a valuation function which assigns 0.68 to a sentence also assigns 0.7 to it. V would not be a function in this case and the idea of a sentence having one truth-value rather than another would collapse. It does not make sense therefore to suppose that the valuation function V assigns anything but 1 to metalinguistic truth assertions.

Rolf's argument shows that it is not possible to give an account of higher order vagueness which would be useful for our purposes. It does not establish that it is not possible to give any account of higher order vagueness within a fuzzy logic account. It might be argued that a language which had an operator D (to be read as "it is definitely the case that") could contain a kind of higher order vagueness for which a logic of degrees of truth would be appropriate. When A is a statement which is assigned a high degree of truth the statement DA is also assigned an appropriately high degree - though not as high as the assignment to A itself - and the statement IA ("it is indefinite that A") is assigned a low degree. D-A is assigned an even lower degree. Sanford presents an account of such a determinacy operator in [2] (p.34). He decides, somewhat arbitrarily, that the assignment of a certain degree of truth to A should determine the assignment to DA according to the formula

$$/DA/ = 1 - 4 \text{ times } /-A/ \text{ when } /A/ \text{ is} \geq 0.75,$$

$$/DA/ = 0 \text{ when } /A/ < 0.75.$$

Assignments to DA and IA are not to be understood as assessments of the accuracy of the original assignment to A or of the amount of uncertainty which attaches to one rather than another assignment to it for we might be very uncertain of an assignment of 0.9 to a statement. /DA/ would in this case be low, but on Sanford's account it would be 0.96. So it is clear that this account goes no way towards solving the problems discussed above.

(b) The Specification Space Approach

In a language which is not vague at all no predicates will have borderline cases. All statements are either definitely true or definitely false. (Or at least if some are not so, the failing is not to be blamed on vagueness.) Assuming there are no truth-value gaps from other sources, there will be just one admissible specification and it will be complete. Let us call a language *first order vague* if, for some of its predicates, there is a class of borderline cases. Natural languages are first order vague since there is uncertainty about whether or not some things are contained within the scope of their predicates. But it seems that the limits of the range of borderline cases are also uncertain. If, as Frege thought, there are no sharp boundaries to be found here, the borderline cases will fade into the clear cases of a predicate's application at one end of the range and the clear cases of its non-application at the other. There will be some dubiously borderline objects: borderline cases of borderline cases.

Fine thinks the existence of borderline cases of borderline cases warrants the introduction of an operator "D" ("it is definitely true that") to distinguish definitely borderline cases from indefinitely borderline ones. "I" is defined by

IA = -DA & -D-A.

Some things are only dubiously borderline. So as well as the definitely indefinite statements, there are two classes of indefinitely borderline ones: those only indefinitely definitely true (but definitely not false), and those indefinitely definitely false (but definitely not true). So there will be five classes of statements -

DDA, IDA, DIA, ID-A, DD-A

- at the second level of vagueness, nine at the third and so on.

Where a language is second order vague there is to be more than one specification space. The idea is that while there is no uniquely correct set of admissible complete specifications for a second order vague language, there is an appropriate set of appropriate sets of such specifications. DDA holds iff A is supertrue at every space within the set; IDA iff A is supertrue at some, superfalse at none; ID-A iff A is superfalse at some and supertrue at none, etc. Doubts might arise about the limits of this set of sets; in that case the language is third order vague, and what is needed is a set of sets of sets. Further uncertainty is accommodated by the same move. In general, an nth order boundary is defined as sequence S_0, S_1, S_2,...,S_n of spaces, each of which contains the preceding space. Dϕ is true at a boundary B iff ϕ is true for all admissible ways of drawing the boundaries within B. If higher order vagueness comes to an end somewhere there is a boundary B_m such that $B_{m+1} = B_m$. It is not clear however, exactly how this works at levels higher than two. For while a space has a structure determined by the base point (the point of which all the other specification points are extensions) there does not seem to be any structural difference between a set of spaces and a set of sets of spaces.

Nor is it clear what the logic of a system containing a D-operator should be. Fine points out an analogy between D and the modal operator L. When considering truth conditions for a language with a D operator the question to consider, he says, is whether the logic is T or something stronger. He decides at one point that it will be S5, though later in the article appears to prefer T after all. (See Fine [1], p.290 and p.294.) T has as axioms

$$Lp \to p$$

and $$L(p \to q) \to (Lp \to Lq)$$

as well as some axioms of the propositional calculus. Intuition does seem to support the corresponding principles:

$$DA \to A$$

is surely true.

The system S4 contains, in addition to the axioms of T, the more controversial

$$Lp \to LLp.$$

Again, intuitions may be found to support the corresponding principle

$$DA \to DDA,$$

for "D" is naturally read as excluding uncertainty. If there is no uncertainty about the truth status of A, it seems that it could not be the case that IDA. Therefore, if A is definitely true, 'definitely A' is definitely true also.

But the interdefinability of D and I would seem to make T and S5 the only options. (If DA implies DDA then surely IA implies DIA.) In the system S5 all modal characteristics are possessed necessarily. As well as the axioms of T and S4 it has

$$Mp \to LMp.$$

However, the corresponding principle

$$IA \to DIA$$

does not seem so plausible on the natural reading suggested above. Where there is uncertainty about the truth status of A it may or may not be the case that DIA. For the uncertainty may concern whether A is definitely true or not and if so, IIA cannot be excluded. In fact it seems possible to harbour doubts about an assignment of either D or I to a statement. T may therefore be the best candidate for the logic of a language containing a D operator.

At any rate, Fine's equivocation between T and S5 reflects an uncertainty he feels over the question of whether higher order vagueness terminates at some point. On the one hand, he thinks it is unnatural to call a halt at any point to the increasing orders of vagueness. For if the levels of vagueness do cease somewhere then *all* vagueness is in a sense eliminable: each vague sentence could be replaced by a perfectly precise sentence preceded by D which would entail the original. Connexions on penumbra would be lost, for the point of assigning I to sentences like "b is red" and "b is pink" is to leave things uncertain.

On the other hand, Fine thinks that the demand for a perfectly precise metalanguage is in line with the classical truth conditions for which he has argued.

What we require is that the true/false/indefinite trichotomy be relatively firm. Ideally, the truth of the disjunction "A is true, false or indefinite" should imply the truth of one of its disjuncts. (Fine [1], p.297.)

The only alternative, he says, to the view that the metalanguage is perfectly precise is to suppose that the set of admissible specifications is intrinsically vague. In this case there would, he thinks, "be a very intimate connexion between vague language and reality" since the truth predicate would be vague.

The consequences of supposing that the set of admissible specifications (in all appropriate spaces) is vague seem disastrous for the supertruth approach. A vague statement is supertrue in a space iff it is true for all ways countenanced in that space of making its constituents precise, definitely true iff it is supertrue in all spaces etc. But it seems that it would always be possible to argue for one more (or one less) admissible specification. An account of truth conditions dependent on there being some fixed set of these could not respect vagueness. The reason why this problem cannot be overcome by shifting up a level will be discussed in the following section.

(c) The Generation of Higher Order Vagueness

Does higher order vagueness terminate at some point? If it does, what considerations bear on the determination of the upper level? These issues turn upon the way higher order vagueness is envisaged and there appear to be two distinct views of the way in which it might be generated.

On one view, higher orders of vagueness are generated when the attempt to draw sharp limits to the application of predicates is defeated by finding things right on the borderline. At level 0 the division of statements containing a predicate into those which are true and those which are false breaks down when things are found right on the boundary of application of the predicate. A third class of indefinite statements must be countenanced as well as the true and the false. But then borderline cases of borderline cases may be discovered making it difficult to fit certain statements into any of the three classes. Differences between the semantic status of these may be expressed with the help of the D operator, and at this level there are, as we saw, five possibilities. Borderline cases of these might then appear requiring further iterations of "I". In the context of the intensional conception of borderline case vagueness Frege's metaphor might be interpreted as meaning that there is no end to this process, that, for any set of semantic categories, borderline cases can be found right on the boundaries. Then higher order vagueness would have no upper limit, though it might always be correct to prefix "D" to the various iterations of "I" attaching to each statement at every level.

It is often argued that natural language does not suffer from rampant higher order vagueness of this infinite kind because the human power to discriminate difficult cases will run out after some level. It may run out quite quickly, at level 4 for instance: it seems probable we would not be able to tell borderline cases of borderline cases of borderline cases of borderline cases from mere borderline cases of borderline cases of borderline cases. If so, higher order vagueness terminates here, for further distinctions would be without meaning. D may be attached to all assignments at this level making the logic S5. But it is not clear why higher order vagueness should terminate at the limits of direct discrimination of difficult cases. So long as nature supplies continua and we are able to recognize certain cases as intermediate by *some* relevant criteria there seems to be no reason why the hierarchy should come to an end. There is no reason, that is, to tie the semantic status of sentences containing vague predicates to the human power to recognise by direct observation that these cases are borderline.

The alternative way of envisaging the generation of higher order vagueness depends on the possibility of generating doubts at each level about classifications already made. (This may also be seen as an interpretation of Frege's metaphor.) It depends not on the discovery of new problem cases on each boundary, but on the potential for uncertainty about the semantic status of statements already classified in one way or another. Perhaps the boundaries of statements already assigned "I" could have been differently drawn, so as to include (for example) many statements classified as false. Or perhaps reasons might be found for counting as true some of those assigned I. One set of semantic assignments seems as good as another. Boundaries may be shifted around whenever rationales for doing so arise, and since there seems to be no natural limit to the discovery of such rationales, admissibility will be vague.

On the first way of generating higher order vagueness no revisions to semantic assignments which had already been made were contemplated. The discovery of new and difficult cases only generated new sets of boundaries and semantic categories appropriate to them. Higher order vagueness could ascend indefinitely. But on the second interpretation higher order vagueness definitely ceases at the second level. At the first level statements are classified as either true or false. This appears arbitrary in some cases: since we feel we could go either way we assign them I. (All others get a D or D- prefix.) But there are alternative ways of classifying statements assigned to these categories. Any reclassification simply adds to or detracts from the contents of one or other of these categories, it does not generate new ones. Borderline cases of a predicate's application in this sense are not things which definitely fail to fit into either its extension or the extension of its negation: they are things which could with equal justice be put into either. Only things which fall between categories generate the need for new ones.

So revisability itself is not a source of higher order vagueness. Tradeoffs are possible, increasing or decreasing the scope of the predicate "true" for example, at the expense or advantage of the predicates "false" and "is on the borderline". D might be regarded as a metalinguistic predicate, like "true", which attaches to truth ascriptions. There is uncertainty about the limits of possible revisability. Here fine discriminations between locations on a range of difficult cases are not what is wanted. It seems that the statement "Fa is definitely true" may be understood either as excluding uncertainty on the part of the speaker concerning the status of "Fa", or as asserting that a is a clear or central case of F-hood a long way from the borderline cases. For one reason or the other the speaker judges that "Fa" is not likely to be revised - its semantic status is clear. Wherever you draw reasonable boundaries to the extension of the predicate F, a will be included.

But the limits to the class of definite truths may be uncertain. When this dimension of uncertainty is imposed on higher order vagueness from the first source the result is a hierarchy in which there are no clear non-arbitrary limits between admissible and non-admissible specifications. Shifting up to higher levels will not resolve the difficulties which result for supervaluation systems, since uncertainty concerning a statement's revisability cannot be be resolved by such moves.

It is not possible therefore to dispose in this way of the difficulties to do with the uncertainty generated by vague predicates. We shall consider an alternative means of dealing with these problems in section 9.5.

Part II:

THE SORITES PARADOX

Chapter 4

THE PARADOX AND THE INCOHERENCE THESIS

4.1 The Incoherence Thesis

We saw in section 1.1 that the Sorites Paradox arises where the predicates of natural language are vague in the sense Frege depicts in his metaphor of the spatial area with hazy boundaries. Where it is legitimate to draw sharp boundaries to the application of a predicate the Sorites reasoning which leads to the contradictory conclusions outlined in 1.1 will obviously fail. Frege's strong borderline case vagueness does appear to infect at least the observational predicates of natural languages,however, for there appears to be an essential uncertainty about the limits of their application.

In this section we shall introduce a discussion of an argument expounded by Michael Dummett[36] in "Wang's Paradox" and Crispin Wright[37] in "On the Coherence of Vague Predicates" which will occupy much of the rest of this work. It is this argument which appears to support the claim, outlined in section 1.1, that if there is vagueness of this Fregean kind in natural languages the Sorites Paradox must be a genuine irresolvable one. Furthermore, Dummett and Wright argue that vagueness of this sort is an essential feature of those languages - one which is not to be eradicated or simply ignored by any adequate theory about them. The conclusion, that vagueness is both essential to natural languages and a source of incoherence in them, leads inevitably to paradox and contradiction. Wright claims the incoherence arises from conflicting elements in the sense of vague predicates: it seems incompatible with their meanings to draw sharp limits anywhere to their application, but unless limits are drawn somewhere they apply indiscriminately.

If these arguments work they show that there could be no logic for languages containing vague expressions and thus that the

---

36 Dummett [1].

37 Wright [1].

paradox is not to be removed by abandoning one or two familiar logical principles, for vague expressions are ones governed by inconsistent rules. Also, there could be no semantics for such languages, since no consistent set of semantic rules could reasonably be supposed to represent speakers' implicit knowledge of their language. These conclusions seem intolerable since (as we said in 1.1) one task of the philosopher is to make systematic sense of the workings of natural languages and this commits us to dissolving paradoxes of this kind.

The argument may be put in the form of a dilemma: either natural languages do contain expressions vague in Frege's strong borderline case sense, in which case the Sorites Paradox is insoluble, or else they are not genuinely vague at all. Dummett and Wright appear to think that there is no way out of this dilemma for natural languages are undeniably vague in Frege's sense. They not only are vague but must be so for vagueness is an inevitable feature of any language used by creatures with our sensory powers and limitations. The Sorites is an inevitable consequence of this vagueness. Dummett and Wright thus agree with Frege that vagueness is a source of incoherence but disagree with his view that it ought to be eliminated from any language adequate to the expression of thought.

We mentioned earlier that Dummett locates one source of the dilemma in a tension between Frege's view that vagueness is a source of incoherence to be eliminated from a logically perfect language and Wittgenstein's view that vagueness is an essential feature of natural languages and vague languages are perfectly in order as they stand. The degree of regularity and coherence evident in the use of natural languages appears to support Wittgenstein's claims here: my argument in the next few chapters will be that this appearance of coherence is genuine and that coherence can be reconciled with vagueness.

4.2 Wright's Arguments for Tolerance

Wright sets his argument in the context of what he calls "the governing view of language". This apparently unexceptionable thesis has two parts. The first is simply that the correct use of language is determined by a set of rules. The second is a view about the correct methodology for discovering a certain kind of rule: those he calls the *substantial* rules for the use of the language. These are supposed to capture our understanding of the specific sense of expressions and settle questions about their application to particular objects. Unlike more austere semantic rules they could be used to convey knowledge of the use of expressions to novice learners of the language. The methodology recommended by the governing view is simply one of consulting our intuitions and working knowledge of the language from the inside, as users of it. We can, for instance, consider the point of applying an expression, what justifies its application and how it could come to be learned.

Wright does not spell out further details of these substantial rules for the use of predicates of natural languages, but we may suppose that being semantic rules they will match features of the world - properties of objects - with syntactically determined predicative expressions. And if methodological considerations of the kind allowed by the second thesis of the governing view are permitted to decide which these features are, we will have to count as determiners of a predicate's application those properties of things which would be selected for the attention of learners of the use of the predicate, those whose presence would standardly be used to justify its application. In general a property counts as a determiner of the application of a predicate where we would feel that we no longer possessed a grasp of the sense of a predicate were we to suppose that drastic alterations in the object with respect to that property did not force us to withdraw the application to it of that predicate. Such properties are therefore candidate satisfiers of suitable clauses of the substantial semantic rules for that predicate.

Considerations of the kind permitted by the second thesis of the governing view lead, Wright claims, to the conclusion that lack of sharp boundaries is essential to the sense of many expressions. The point of applying predicates such as "loud", "small", "sweet", "old", "red" etc. - predicates Wright calls observational - is to characterize things according to the way they appear to ordinary observers on casual examination. Observational predicates are, for Wright, ones standardly applied in this way, without recourse to counting or measurement or the use of instruments. The object of this argument is to establish that we could not use observational predicates as we do - to characterize things according to the way they appear - if two things could be indistinguishable to the senses and yet one but not the other deserve a predicate of this sort. So if they appear the same to normal observers in the conditions in which the predicate is usually applied and the predicate applies to one it applies to the other also.

Since there are limits to our powers of sensory discrimination there are bound to be real physical differences between things which are too small to notice. But minute differences too small to be detected cannot affect the applicability of a predicate standardly applied at a casual glance. We must conclude, he says, that these predicates are *tolerant to marginal change*: their applicability always survives some small degree of real alteration in relevant respects. Size is certainty a determining feature for the predicate "heap", yet a heap remains a heap when its size is diminished by some small amount. So "heap" is a tolerant predicate. Very small lapses of time make no difference to the applicability of the predicates "child" and "adult", though in each case larger differences of the same kind would alter their applicability. The application of the predicate "bald" survives the growth of a hair or two, though quantity of hair is what determines its application and larger gains of this kind would make the predicate inapplicable. Where a predicate is tolerant in this sense there are changes too small ever to matter.

These conclusions might be claimed to follow from any view on which questions about meaning are not to be divorced from considerations to do with the conditions under which expressions are usually applied and standardly learned for the first time. For predicates such as "red" and "child" are learned ostensively. It would not be possible to learn them in this way, Wright claims, if differences too small to be noticed or clearly remembered by the novice language-learner affected their applicability. Ostensive training is fully determinative of the meaning of such predicates, according to Wright, or is at least the only training in their use that we get.

He thinks we are also led to the conclusion that these predicates are tolerant by considering the consequences of their use in each case. Predicates such as "child" and "adult" carry implications about socially important rights and duties, and it would be unfair to make differences in their applicability depend on changes too slight to be obvious. The conclusion must be that if one of these predicates applies to some person it must also apply to any other who is indistinguishable from the first in terms of appearance with respect to physical maturity. To stipulate away the tolerance of predicates such as "child" would, he claims, conflict with the social importance we attach to these labels. So to deny that observational predicates are tolerant is to deny their whole point: their consequences and the rationale for their use. It would also, he says, give a false picture of the language: a picture of a language we could not use.

Let us say, adopting some more of Wright's terminology, that a concept ϕ *determines the application of a predicate F* when there are changes in objects with respect to ϕ which make F applicable to them, and other changes in them with respect to ϕ which make F no longer applicable. We can then say that a predicate is tolerant when there are alterations with respect to the determining concepts for the predicate which are too small to ever alter its applicability. (This dubious terminology of concepts is not strictly necessary to Wright's statement of the argument, for if the view of his substantial rules for the application of predicates which was spelled out above is correct, talk of concepts could be replaced throughout by talk of properties.)

Non-observational predicates are not tolerant with respect to marginal changes in their determining concepts. The predicate "six feet and two and a half inches tall" is not tolerant, since any alteration in the length of a thing to which this predicate applied would transport it outside the scope of the predicate's application. But if the above considerations count, *strict tolerance rules* such as the following seem to be part of the sense of all observational predicates:

> If one thing is a heap and a second has just one less grain, the second is a heap also.
>
> If one person is bald and a second has one more hair than the first, the second is bald also.
>
> If one person is a child then any other indistinguishable from the first in terms of apparent maturity is a child also.

Wright has one further argument for tolerance to do with predicates which he calls *purely observational*. These are predicates whose applicability to objects is always to be decided just by the use of the senses. If a predicate's application is determined on these grounds alone - by the way the thing looks or sounds or feels or smells etc. - then no other considerations could be allowed to undermine the judgement made about it by a competent observer. The argument is that these predicates at least must be tolerant, even if no others are. For if casual observers are to be the final arbiters, any things they cannot tell apart must be judged the same, that is, as deserving of the same predicate. So if any predicate of this purely observational sort applies to one of a pair of things indistinguishable to the senses it must apply to the other also.

And so Wright's arguments for toleranceare further arguments for the existence in natural language of the kind of haziness about boundaries which we have been calling Fregean vagueness. The object of his arguments is to establish that we could not use observational predicates in the way we do - to characterize things according to the way they appear - if they were not tolerant of marginal changes in determining respects. If two things are indistinguishable to the senses and one deserves an observational predicate, then the other does also. There may be a small difference between the two of a kind which, if it were larger, would justify applying the predicate to one but not the other, but since the predicate is tolerant there is some degree of difference too small ever to matter. So if a pair of things appear the same to normal observers in the conditions in which an observational predicate is usually applied and the one object deserves the predicate, then the other must deserve it also. Where there is tolerance there can be no sharp boundaries and so there will be vagueness of the Fregean kind.

But where predicates are tolerant and therefore vague in this sense it seems that there is no escape from the paradox. If removing a single grain from a heap always leaves us with a heap we can be forced by many small steps to apply the predicate to things which are mere pinches, or even to no grains at all. And if in general a man with only one more hair than a bald man is bald also, we are driven to conclude that all men are bald. Worse, we must admit that no-one is bald. It can be proved in this manner that everyone is and is not a child as well as tall and short, middle-aged and over-weight, and also youthful and slender.

All observational predicates are essentially vague since they must be tolerant. The conditions under which they are applied are such that no sharp boundaries can be drawn to delimit their field of application. Clear cases of the application and non-application of such a predicate could always be linked by intermediate cases which are indiscernible in the respects that matter to observers applying the predicate in normal conditions. There could be no justification for applying an observational predicate to one such case and not to the next, since the predicates are applied on the basis of the way things appear on casual inspection and they would appear the same in those circumstances. So vagueness is both an essential feature of natural languages and an incoherent one.

4.3 Versions of the Paradox

In "Wang's Paradox" Dummett sets out a version of the Sorites paradox which goes as follows:

> 0 is a small number
> If some number n is small then its successor is small
> Therefore every number is small.

The conclusion is false, at least on some natural interpretations of "small". However the first premiss is true on these interpretations and the second seems very plausible also. To deny it is to assert that there are sharp limits to the application of the vague predicate "small" but this would involve denying that it is vague in Frege's sense. If both premisses are accepted the conclusion follows by weak mathematical induction. Dummett considers various ways in which the appearance of paradox might be removed, some of which we shall discuss below.

The general form of the argument can be represented as a mathematical induction on the property expressed by some predicate F which is true of some things at one end of a series S and false of things at the other end. It may be stated as follows:

(i) If any arbitrarily chosen member n of S is F, then the next member, n+1, is F also

(ii) The first member of the series is F

Therefore,

(iii) Every member of S is F.

We supposed however that F was false of things at one end of the series. We could establish by the same form of argument that the predicate -F applied to all members of the series including the first.

The same contradictory conclusions can be derived by using a chain of arguments involving individual steps of Modus Ponens. Starting from the first member of the series, we argue that this member is F, and if this is F, so is the next. At the next stage we use the conclusion that the second member is F and the conditional that if the second is F, so is the third. We can argue in this way that every member of the series is F.

A different kind of reasoning is used in an example by Cargile.[38] A camera, focused on a tadpole in a bowl of water, runs continuously for three weeks at a rate of 24 frames per second. At the end of three weeks there are 43,545,600 pictures which can be arranged in a series in the order taken. Where P is the property of being the number of a picture of a tadpole, P clearly applies to the first picture but not the last. Cargile offers a proof that there must be some n such that (P(n) & -P(n+1)), making use of the least number principle in the form:

If the number 1 has a property and a larger number n does not, there is a least number between 1 and n which does not have the property.

This seems paradoxical since it implies that the creature is a tadpole in one picture and not the next - 1/24th of a second later. Given what we know of tadpolehood and froghood we would be inclined to say that there is no n such that (P(n) & -P(n+1)).

Finally, Unger makes use of a version of the Sorites to argue for the radically sceptical position that ordinary things do not exist. He locates the source of the paradox in a conflict between science and common sense. His argument in [2] proceeds by *reductio ad absurdum* from the assumption that ordinary things, such as stones or tables, exist. He claims the following propositions form an inconsistent set:

(1) There is at least one stone.

(2) For anything there may be, if it is a stone, then it consists of many atoms, but a finite number.

(3) For anything there may be, if it is a stone, then the net removal of one atom, in a way which is most innocuous and favourable, will not mean the difference as to whether there is a stone in the situation.

Unger claims that only the first premiss can be rejected. We shall discuss his version of the arguement in detail in later sections.

4.4 An Empirical Assumption

All these versions of the paradox outlined in the last section have in common the notion of a series of things ordered with respect to

---

38 Cargile [1].

their possession of certain features, or the degree to which they possess them. These features are of a kind which determines the applicability of a predicate of natural language, and the argument is designed to project the property expressed by that predicate from members of the series which clearly possess the property to ones which clearly do not. In either case the argument makes an assumption which will be discussed later in some detail. It assumes that it is always possible to find appropriate objects and arrange them in a series of a suitable sort. Starting with someone clearly not bald, we envisage a series of men, each with one less hair than the next, until we end up with someone who is completely hairless. Alternatively, we could imagine separate stages of a single person who loses a hair at each stage. Another example consists of homogeneously coloured strips, each so similar in shade to the next that they seem to form a continuous band of colour ranging from red through to orange. The first is clearly red and the last clearly orange but the variation in shade is so gradual that each would be judged indistinguishable in shade from its immediate neighbours. This is an empirical assumption, but it appears to be a safe one to make. It would seem at least possible that appropriate objects could always be found and arranged in an apparently continuous series.

It is only if this assumption about the availability of suitable series is accepted that the Sorites argument can be represented as a mathematical induction on the property expressed by some observational predicate F. To present the argument in this way it must be assumed that S is a series of the kind just outlined, and the predicate F is true of things at one end of the series and false of things at the other. It must also be supposed that the size of the difference from member to member in the determining respect for F is within the limits of tolerance for that predicate. It seems that all the versions of the paradox rest on these empirical assumptions.

It seems to be generally agreed that the empirical assumptions on which these arguments rest cannot seriously be doubted. It is hard to imagine reasons why suitable objects could not, in principle, be found and arranged to form appropriate series. For we can easily imagine a large heap becoming smaller by imperceptible degrees as grains (or parts of grains) are removed one grain (or atom) at a time. And there are, it seems, actual examples of such series in nature where small variations, impossible to detect over a short period of time, may add up to a large difference over a long stretch of time. The effect of wear and tear, and weather is to produce changes of just this kind. There seems in these cases to be no room for doubt that such series would present an appearance of smoothly continuous change.

4.5 Dummett's View of the Paradox

The source of the paradox is, according to Dummett, the non-transitivity of the relation "not discernibly different from". There may be some triad of things, a, b and c, where a is indiscernible from b in some respect of superficial appearance such as shade of colour, and b is indiscernible from c in the same respect, but it is just possible to discern a difference in this respect between a and c. Given the continuity of the world and the finite nature of human perceptual abilities, indiscernibility is bound to be a non-transitive relation. This is, he thinks, what makes the paradox inevitable. Any language devised by creatures with our perceptual limitations would be bound to contain expressions whose application conditions were insensitive to small alterations in determining respects: yet many small changes may add up to a difference to which we are sensitive.

Dummett's diagnosis of the paradox brings out an interesting connexion with another puzzle often used to try to refute sense data theorists. Suppose these three statements are all true:

(1) a and b appear to observer O to be the same shade of colour all over
(2) b and c appear to O to be the same shade of colour all over
(3) a and c appear to O to be just discernibly different shades of colour all over.

Is it possible to avoid the conclusion that b appears to be two distinct shades of colour all over its surface at the same time? [39]

Dummett's response to this puzzle is the same as his answer to the versions of the Sorites set out above. It is also the obvious one, (except to sense data theorists): there can be no phenomenal properties. For if there were they would be determined solely by our powers of discrimination, and these powers do not determine consistent sets of things. To show that a property is incoherent is to show that it does not exist. So if colours are phenomenal properties, there are no colours. If which things are heaps is

[39] We discuss this paradox in chapter 8.

determined by the appearance of things, there are no heaps. There are only physical properties of things.

This response does not resolve any of the problems in which we are interested. It depends upon the thesis that natural language is fundamentally incoherent, and so leaves us with the puzzle of how we are able to understand that language and use it as consistently as we do. It also leaves us with the Sorites Paradox, since this puzzle now appears inevitable so long as we do continue to understand and use observational language.

4.6 *Ad Hoc* Stipulation and Inconsistent Rules

Wright's arguments for tolerance seem to leave one residual puzzle. What are we to make of the fact that we do manage to limit the applicability of these observational predicates, that they are not in fact applied indiscriminately? When, in practice, the need to precisify a vague predicate arises, we simply stipulate boundaries in an *ad hoc* manner. Town planners announce that a certain population is to constitute a city, geographers prescribe limits to the scope of the words "mountain" and "tributary". And in many ordinary situations non-philosophers seem content to accept the same sort of *ad hoc* stipulation. Quine argued in "What Price Bivalence"[40] that this way of dealing with the problems presented by vague predicates accords with scientific practice as well as good sense. All this seems to be evidence that there are elements in the sense of observational predicates which allow sharp boundaries to be drawn.

This is not taken by Wright and Dummett to be an objection to their argument. In fact it is absorbed into the argument that natural languages are essentially incoherent. For if, as they claim, tolerance principles are *also* essential to the sense of observational predicates it seems that their meanings must contain inconsistent and conflicting elements. We are forced by some elements in their sense to disallow sharp boundaries and permitted by others to stipulate sharp limits in a fairly arbitrary fashion. To the question of how we could possibly operate with such conflicting rules the only possible answer would seem to be the one Wright suggests: that we do so inconsistently. Since individuals are capable of adopting contradictory beliefs from time to time and changing the rules when it suits them, it seems just possible that the whole language-using population might have accepted a set of inconsistent linguistic rules. Then natural languages would

---

40 Quine [3],pp.92f.

contain deeply embedded inconsistencies and the Sorites would be an insoluble paradox.

The idea that ordinary language might be *mildly* inconsistent in places is not too implausible. For as we noted in section 1.7, there seems to be a certain "looseness of fit" about many observational predicates. Some people find "green" an appropriate description of the colour of some objects which other people call blue. But the idea that there is *massive* incoherence of the sort Dummett and Wright suggest appears to be incompatible with the degree of consistency which is evident in this part of the language. Not only do we apply the predicates discriminately - to some objects and not to others - but we manage to coincide to quite a large extent with one another in applying and withholding them where we do. This seems hard to explain if, as Wright is claiming, we are arbitrarily selecting inconsistent rules. It would be sheer accident that there is this much agreement over the description of particular objects. So how else are we to explain our coinciding to the extent we do in applying and withholding observational predicates if we are not to suppose that we are guided in some systematic way by a coherent set of rules and principles?

This objection to the incoherence thesis may also surface when the above argument about the observation of apparently continuous series is examined more closely. For we know that anyone observing a series of gradually varying things will find it appropriate to apply certain observational predicates to some of the members but not to all of them. At some point they will hesitate perhaps, and then refuse to apply some predicate to any further members despite having applied it to all the previous ones. Different observers may baulk at different points, but these points will surely all be within some small range. The limits of this range could presumably be roughly determined by testing a large enough sample of normal users of the language. We could then predict that other potential observers of this series, outside of our sample, would also limit the scope of their predicates to some point within this roughly delimited range. It seems unlikely that the drawing of boundaries to the application of predicates could be as predictable as this if there were no further systematic means of resolving the apparently conflicting elements in their meanings.

This problem might appear to be almost as great a difficulty for Quine's moderate common-sense approach as it is for the view that there is massive incoherence in natural language. It is just as difficult to account for the degree of consistency that exists in our drawing of limits to the application of observational predicates if it is supposed to be a totally *ad hoc* and arbitrary matter that we draw them where we do, as it is to explain it on the supposition that we are following conflicting rules.

4.7 Causal Explanations of Consistency

A common reply is available to both Quine and Wright, some details of which might be filled in by considering some of Quine's writings on other topics related to perception. The degree of consistency which is evident in the application of observational predicates invites a causal explanation. Such an explanation, using laws of appropriate physical theories, would be compatible with both Quine's views and the incoherence thesis. From the point of view of the users of language their decisions about the application or non-application of vague predicates are bound to seem *ad hoc* when they are confronted with borderline case objects. It is only from the point of view of the external scientific observer of the language-using community that any consistency is evident. The set of physical laws which determine the application or non-application of the predicate to an object are not rules which language users could employ in order to decide the status of a description of some object. They are left, therefore, without any coherent rationale for their decisions.

To give the cause of a stipulated boundary to the application of some predicate is not to provide a justification for drawing it there: a causal explanation of what language users do will not be an account of systematic and communally accepted guiding rules and principles. (Of course the latter might be a variety of causal explanation, but this has no bearing on the question at issue here. For the kind of causal account in which we are interested is obviously not available to ordinary users of the language as a rationale for their applying predicates as they do.) So the objection to the incoherence thesis which rested upon the evidence for consistency in usage may be met, and that thesis strengthened, by the addition to the story of some causal explanation of our agreement over the application of observational predicates.

How might such a causal explanation run? One plausible way would involve filling out the picture of the observer's psychological states. Their concentration and interest in the proceedings are bound to vary from moment to moment, as will their expectation about what is about to be seen. We could imagine that some group of patches at which an observer glances all look red and then, a moment later, when they attend carefully, the next lot all look orange. The last member of the first lot might be adjacent to the first patch in the second group.

An account of this sort does not yet explain why we all agree pretty well that these are orange and those red. A further explanation, familiar from Quine's writing on natural kinds[41] would be that we all coincide roughly in our application and non-application of colour predicates because of shared similarities in quality spacing. Similarities in boundaries of this kind would surely account for coincidences within a certain range of observers' hesitating, applying and withholding the application of observational predicates.

Some variation from one observer to the next is to be expected since individuals' habits and histories of word learning deviate. Also, their concentration will wander at different moments. So the claim is that it could in principle be predicted from an experimentally tested theory that a human observer will draw a sharp boundary (falling within a certain range) to the applicability of an observational predicate in a particular context. Different observers draw the line in different places within the range for psychological reasons unknown to them.

4.8 Wright's Conclusions

There seems to be no reason why a causal explanation of the kind suggested in the last section, making use of the laws of appropriate physical theories and the hypothesis of similarities in quality-spacing, could not account for the fact that an observer of a Sorites series will apply a predicate up to some point, then hesitate and refuse to project it to any further members. There need be no inconsistency in such an account from an external point of view of what determines the application and non-application of observational predicates. In fact, the moral Wright draws from the whole argument about tolerance is that it is only from this behaviouristic external viewpoint that sense can be made of the language. The governing view is to be rejected.

This seems an unsatisfactory conclusion. Having persuaded us (perhaps) that there are inconsistent elements in the sense of the words we use, he tries to tell us to adopt a different methodology, one which will not lead to these impossible conclusions. This involves closing our eyes to the appearance of

---

41 See 'Natural Kinds' in Quine [2].

things as well as to our knowledge of the sense of the words we use. It is just too difficult to reject the belief that there is some non-behavioural component to understanding which (at least in part) accounts for our success in communication. This objection to the rejection of the second thesis of the governing view is somewhat unclear, and we shall attempt to sharpen it up in succeeding chapters. A more serious ground for concern at this stage is simply that we have been given no reason to think tolerance rules false, just told to ignore them. And no matter how they may be discovered, if tolerance rules are true (that is if they are involved in the sense of the words we use), then the paradox seems inevitable.

Also, even if it were possible to take the above considerations as good grounds for rejecting tolerance rules, the difficulty is not resolved. There are other paradoxes which seem to involve essentially the same problem, but where the contradictory consequences can be derived without making use either of considerations to do with tolerance or of any special knowledge available just to users of the language. There is, for instance, the puzzle outlined above in 4.5 which has been used to argue against sense datum theories of perception.

Wright's rejection of the second thesis of the governing view entails more than a revision of the methodolgy used to uncover the rules determining the use of natural language. The recommended behaviouristic stance alters the thesis that the use of language is governed by rules, since the character of those rules can be no different from that of the laws of any empirical theory. There are no specifically "semantic" rules.[42]

Wright's rejection of the governing view is usually taken as a rejection of a certain view of meaning and understanding: the view that there is some inner introspectible component to our understanding of an expression and that this may be expressed in the form of rules known to speakers and used in forming judgements about objects. The application of observational predicates is thought, on this view, to be governed by rules speakers use, in contrast with rules which simply determine speakers' application of observational predicates in the way laws of nature determine the behaviour of inanimate objects.

---

42 This interpretation of Wright's conclusions is based upon my reading of Wright [2] in which he attacks Davidson's claims that axiomatic systems meeting certain formal constraints may provide a formal theory of meaning for a natural language.

Though this is the moral often drawn from a consideration of Wright's arguments[43] there does not appear to be any genuine tension between these two views about rules. Wright's arguments do not seriously undermine the plausibility of the view that there are rules known in some sense to users of the language - guidelines employed when judging whether predicates such as "bald" and "red" apply to objects - and there appears to be no reason why the use of such rules should put us outside the scope of deterministic laws. His arguments do not force us to choose between these views or to reject the view of meaning and understanding with which he starts out. To do so might be a way of ignoring the paradox (or at least most versions of it), but is clearly not a satisfactory resolution of it.

---

43 See, for instance, Platts [1], pp.217-218

Chapter 5

REPONSES TO THE PARADOX

Having discussed in the last chapter Dummett and Wright's views of the Sorites Paradox and their responses to the arguments for the incoherence thesis we shall consider here some responses of other philosophers to the two puzzles. The strategy in this chapter is as follows: we shall first discuss some of the usual ways of attempting to deal with the Sorites Paradox to be found in the literature, showing how Wright's and Dummett's arguments bear on these, and secondly, we shall discuss the few attempts to directly confront their arguments for the incoherence thesis. (There will of course be some overlap here: some of those who have been aware of Wright's and Dummett's arguments have also proposed ways out of the Sorites.) The conclusion will be that if Wright's and Dummett's arguments are correct we are forced to reject the former attempts to solve the Sorites, and further, that none of the latter attempts to avoid the conclusions of their arguments succeed.

5.1 The Elimination of Vagueness

> "We are confronted with the imaginary spectacle of a people quite lost without their wheelbarrow loads of charts, tape-recorders, smell- and taste-samples and assorted sample surfaces." (Wright [1], p.358.)

If language contained no vague terms the Sorites Paradox and all the associated difficulties discussed in the last chapter would not arise. It is sometimes suggested that wholesale revision of the language, purifying it of all vagueness, provides the only way out of these problems. Frege is often thought to have recommended this course. It seems, however, that Frege's remarks about vagueness are often intended, as Dummett says,[43] to get it out of the way, so as to discuss the construction of a formal language free of this defect. And so it seems that he

---

43 Dummett [4], pp.32-3.

should not be taken as literally suggesting semantic revision of the languages in which Sorites paradoxes can arise.

One philosopher who appears to have seriously proposed this exercise in prescriptive semantics as a means of resolving the Sorites Paradox is Unger. The recommended reform would consist in laying down exactly the boundaries of application of such ordinary words as "cow", "red" and "loud". In some cases precise quantities might be used in these definitions (such as numbers of atoms, or wavelengths of reflected light or of sound), in others samples might be used as standards in the way the standard metre is used to determine the application of certain predicates of length. Hence the need for the wheelbarrow.

However, Wright argues that the consequences of the proposal are not as comic as might at first appear. Once trained in the new application conditions we could dispense with the wheelbarrow for all practical purposes. We could learn to tell in most cases just by observation whether or not something is a heap without having to resort to counting grains. Provided suitable sharp definitions were chosen the revision would have no practical effect on the use of language since it would only make a difference in cases at present judged borderline.

The main objection to this proposal as a means of resolving the Paradox is simply that it will never be carried out. Just saying that our concept of a stone or a wombat is to be precise does not make it so. It is not at all clear who Unger thinks should undertake the task of prescriptive semantics but it is obvious that their efforts would be in vain and so would be no reform of the language at all. And the knowledge that the recommended reforms would go unheeded by the general public will no doubt discourage anyone from trying.

5.2 Ideal Languages, Logic and Precision

Quine argues in [3] that we needn't worry about vagueness in natural language so long as we have available an ideal scientific language free of vagueness. Paradoxes like the Sorites arise, he says, because of the existence of observational terms in natural language and to solve them we need only "work the requisite precision into the vague terms that we learned by ostension" (Quine [3], p.92.) There is a two stage process: what had been observation terms are arbitrarily reconstrued, on pain of paradox, as theoretical terms whose application may depend in marginal cases on protracted tests and indirect inferences. Vagueness does not matter, he claims, so long as an ideal language is available, in the sense that we could in principle construct it were we motivated to do so.

It is not clear why the mere ability to create a language free of observational terms shows the problem to be non-existent. If Wright's arguments hold this ability to draw arbitrary limits to the application of vague terms when it suits us is part of the evidence for the incoherence of natural language, for it is inconsistent with the tolerance rules which are part of the sense of those terms. Since the ideal tolerance-free language could not replace the vastly more convenient natural one whose terms may be applied on the basis of casual observation it does not seem that the problem can be made to disappear in the way Quine suggests.

Various grounds have been suggested for arguing that vague expressions and sentences are outside the scope of logic. If this were so it might be possible to remove the appearance of paradox and avoid the other difficulties discussed in the last chapter by arguing that the principles used to derive the unwanted conclusions simply do not apply to vague natural languages.

Jeffrey, in *Formal Logic; Its Scope and Limits*, has the following suggestion for rescuing language from the threat of paradox. There are some circumstances in which sentences which are uttered fail to make statements. Jeffrey claims that the application of a predicate to one of its borderline cases is one such circumstance. Failures of presupposition are another such case. Both result in a sentence without a truth value: logic is only concerned with sentences which have truth values, and so the principles of logic do not lead to the paradoxical conclusions described above.

This suggestion does not seem to rescue us from the paradox. Vague predicates have clear applications and so can be used to make true (and false) statements. So, for example, the first premiss of Dummett's version of the Sorites reasoning must be true. No argument seems to have been advanced against the second premiss (or against the induction step in the generalized version of the paradox) and so it must be assumed to be true also. (In favour of accepting it as a truth guaranteed by the meanings of vague predicates we have Wright's and Dummett's arguments rehearsed in the last chapter. If they are right, abandoning the induction step as not true would mean abandoning part of the meaning of vague predicates.) So we have the paradox still.

Also, the refusal to apply the principles of logic to vague languages seems the wrong response to the Paradox for several reasons. There are surely better and worse arguments couched in natural language involving vague terms. We want to know where the Sorites argument goes wrong. Jeffrey's type of response ignores the challenge to make systematic sense of our intuitions concerning which natural language arguments are good and which bad. Secondly, there appears to be no reason why logic should not apply to statements which are neither true nor false (or not definitely true or false.) If the existence of such statements is a consequence of vagueness, then it must be determined which is the best account of a language containing vague terms. Should such a language be regarded as containing truth value gaps? Or should its semantics incorporate multiple truth values? Systems claiming to be logics have been provided to accommodate these alternatives. There appear to be no grounds, therefore, for the claim that vague statements are outside the bounds of logic.

It is sometimes argued that *no* statements of natural language are true or false (or no statements involving vague terms.) This view escapes the reply to Jeffrey just given because if no statements of natural language are true the two premisses of the Sorites reasoning (in the mathematical induction version) are not true. Where the premisses of an argument are not true we need not accept its conclusion even though we may admit that the argument is valid. Since this way out of the Paradox could be used by someone who believed the principles of classical logic *did* apply to natural languages it is of no concern to us here and will be discussed below in section 5.4.

Other grounds, apart from those offered by Jeffery, may be found for claiming that logic is inapplicable to languages which contain vague terms. It is often claimed (by Russell and Frege among others) that classical logic assumes precision. This assumption is sometimes thought to surface in the Principle of Bivalence or the Law of Excluded Middle (see Putnam [2], for example), and to regard either of these as necessary truths is it is claimed to overlook vagueness. Hence, classical logic assumes precision and where terms are not precise it simply fails to apply. Since natural language abounds in vague terms the province of logic is just ideal languages of the kind with which Frege, Russell and Quine are concerned.

We saw above, in chapters 1 and 3, that there is a plausible interpretation of vagueness on which it is compatible with both ExM and Biv. If this is so, some alternative account needs to be given of the sense in which logic assumes precision, if this is to be taken as ground for arguing that it does not apply to vague languages. Black argues in [2] that logic presupposes precise concepts in the sense that it embodies the assumption that the concepts used in the sentences to which it is applied admit of no uncertain or unclear cases. This assumption must be admitted to be false, but the situation here is no worse, Black claims, than that of any scientific theory and its empirical interpretation. Thermodynamics assumes its perfect gases and geometry its ideal lines. These theories do not really apply to the world but are near enough to true and give roughly the right answer. The principles of logic may be applied to sentences containing vague terms with the same reservations. He suggests further that they might be seen one day as points of departure for more elaborate laws of which they are just a special limiting case.

This analogy used here seems wrong. The application of logic to vague expressions leads not to roughly true conclusions but to outright contradictions. There does not seem to be any way of applying the laws of logic "with care", as Black recommends, which will enable us to avoid the conclusions of the Sorites.

5.3 Rejecting Common Sense

> "First, we may suppose the existence of heaps. Secondly, we note that, if any heap exists, it consists of various other entities - of grains of sand, or of beans, for example. Finally, we note that, if one bean is removed without replacement, and this is done most favourably and innocuously, what remains will be a heap. Thus, given anything like our view of reality, heaps, which many suppose to be ordinary existing things, are only fictions: there are no heaps". (Unger [2], pp.248-249.)

Unger makes use of Sorites arguments to defend the radically sceptical and nihilistic position that ordinary things do not exist. He claims that the right response to the paradox is to accept it as genuine and that this is the inevitable conclusion which must be drawn. Unlike Wright, who locates the problem in an incoherence in language as used by creatures with limited perceptual capacities, Unger assumes language to be in order and locates the source of the paradox in a conflict between science and commonsense. The world view of commonsense is wrong, he claims, for there are no earth, stars or sun; nor are there trees, tables, typewriters, wombats or people. In one article he courageously draws the final conclusion that he does not exist, and neither does anyone else.

One variety of argument he uses proceeds by *reductio ad absurdum* from the premiss that ordinary things of some sort exist. (See section 4.3 for a brief account of this argument.) What are we left with? There are still, according to Unger, those physical objects countenanced by the exact sciences (excluding astronomy and biology.) He admits that some of these may well exist in the vicinity which is supposed to be inhabited by the non-entities mentioned above but he seems to think that we have no good reason to believe that this is so in any particular instance. This seems quite wrong. If we (incorrectly, according to Unger) believe that a stone exists in some particular place then we will probably have good reason for believing some large number of atoms exists just there. Sorites arguments cannot touch this belief. Given that we have good reason for thinking that there is a large mass of atoms there and that the mass consisting of those atoms behaves in the way we expect stones to behave (or not behave) then it seems hard to deny that there is a stone there. For there is something there which fits our conception of a stone. It seems impossible therefore to accept the Sorites simply as a *reductio* of the ontology of commonsense. The further morals Unger draws from the Sorites have already been discussed in section 5.1.

Other writers have also pointed out that the premisses of the Sorites argument are usually attacked and defended by appeal to commonsense. It has been argued that, as a consequence, the debate bypasses various philosophical theories concerning identity and essentialism, reduction and theory change and reference and meaning which are relevant to the premisses and assumptions involved. It could be claimed that an adequate investigation of these might show that the reply just given to Unger's version of the argument can be met.

Suppose it is claimed that sharp limits may be drawn to a predicate's scope, and the induction step thereby rejected. This need not amount to a proposal to change the meaning of the predicate. The claim might be construed rather as a consequence of the view that meaning is to be divorced from reference. It might be argued therefore,that if we reject the claims of certain theories of reference Sorites problems will not arise. The theories which must be rejected are ones in which the reference of a concept is determined by internal features (its sense.) The reference of a term should instead be decided by external features such as the historical record of its application or scientific theory. The difficulty with this is that it is entirely plausible in the case of vague observational predicates to suppose that their reference *is* determined by internal features - rules adopted by language users or the practice of a majority of users in a community - for there appears to be *nothing else* which might reasonably be supposed to determine that reference. No theoretical considerations can be advanced which might override the intuitions of ordinary users and be used to determine the exact limits of a predicate's scope, for there is no theory to appeal to in the case of most vague observational predicates. And the actual record of their application contains inconsistencies and fails to determine what is to be said about borderline cases.

Nevertheless Wheeler, in [1] and [2], thinks a consideration of the Sorites dilemma shows that we should adopt in place of the internalist theory a causal theory of reference determination. Facts about the sense of natural language predicates do not determine how they are to be applied. So one of a pair of people who differ by one-twentieth of an inch may be tall and the other not. Only the acceptance of internalist theories makes this seem implausible, he claims.

This cannot be right, however, for the vast majority of people who have not heard of the distinction he is making would nevertheless find this consequence implausible. What does determine the application of a concept on Wheeler's view is a theory about its referents. Theories involving the sorts of concepts which have genuine borderline cases are archaic theories, he says, which are literally false. They ought to be rejected because they do not designate kinds. And so statements in such theories, such as "Whitlam is tall", "Peter Garrett is bald", "Ripe tomatoes are red" etc. are all literally false. The fact that we can communicate by means of the archaic theories of the short, the tall, the hot, the cold etc. does not go to show they are true for we understand fiction and falsehood.

This response to the paradox would appear to have the effect of reversing the truth values of most of the statements made with the use of the language if these "literally false" theories are supposed to have false consequences. True statements ("Peter Garrett is bald", "grass is green", "ripe tomatoes are red" etc.) would have to be accounted false. But if a statement is false its negation is true. The absurdity of this seems sufficient grounds for rejecting Wheeler's argument.

There appears, however, to be more than one line of argument being presented in these articles and one of them may escape these absurd consequences. In [2] it seems he does not want to reject the induction step and conclude that the commonsense "theories" which would support it are literally false and have false consequences. It seems his account here might best be construed as claiming that our archaic theories of the hot and cold, short and tall etc. involve presuppositions which are false: they assume that there are such properties and that ordinary things exist whereas the Sorites argument shows that this is not so. There are none of these things because the terms for them fail to designate genuine kinds. Ordinary things such as stones and persons are not kinds, since no genuine scientific laws are true of them. There are, of course, rough rules of thumb but these fail to establish kinds.

Since the prospects for improved theories of the bald, the short and the tall (etc.) are obviously nil we must continue to make sense of natural language predicates. Not to do so, on the grounds of Unger's and Wheeler's arguments, would involve us in more paradoxes. If there are no persons how can the mistaken view that there are have arisen? Both Wheeler and Unger show a preference for *reductio ad absurdum* styles of argument which seems surprising, since their conclusions - that most ordinary terms do not refer that ordinary things do not exist etc. - might be taken as a reductio of the views, about reference, the relation between ordinary ontology and theory, science and common sense etc., on which their arguments rest.

5.4 Rejecting the Induction Step

It is often claimed that there is no paradox because one of the premisses of the above argument, in all of its forms, is false. Hence there is nothing wrong with the actual reasoning. It is usually the induction step of the argument when it is presented as a mathematical induction which is blamed. For Cargile's example it would be the premiss

For all n, if P(n) then P(n+1)

The difficulty about the claim that this is false is that it appears to carry a commitment to the view that there is a value of n such that P(n) and -P(n+1). But which could it be? The problem is not that the choice of any particular number would be arbitrary, but that to choose at all is wrong because it amounts to denying that the predicate P is tolerant. And this amounts as we saw to denying that Fregean vagueness exists. As there is good evidence that language is vague in Frege's sense this way out appears to be blocked.

Nevertheless it seems worthwhile to look in more detail at some of the attempts to escape the paradox by taking this direction, since it is the most popular and occurs to almost everyone when first introduced to the Sorites argument. Cargile argues that the fact that we do not know which picture is the last tadpole picture does not show that there is no fact of the matter. The gradual transition recorded by the camera consists of superficial changes in the appearance of the creature, but what should really count in determining the application of the concept are internal processes not evident on casual inspection. When these are investigated carefully, sharp criteria may be formulated for the application of the predicates of tadpole- and frog-hood. There is a moment when the adrenal glands begin to secrete the hormones which trigger the superficial observable changes and there are points at which certain hormonal levels are reached or interactions occur between chemicals which could reasonably be chosen as sharply delimiting tadpole-hood. That is, there could be some point at which it is plausible for the biologist to say: "Now it's a tadpole, but in this next frame (taken 1/24th of a second later) it's a frog".

This kind of response ceases to be plausible, however, when the the series is more finely gradated. And in the case of other predicates such as "red" and "bald" this type of suggestion could only amount to one or other of the proposals discussed above. If a precise sense were to be assigned to each of the predicates now used to denote phenomenal properties the result would probably be, as Wright points out, the introduction of new predicates designed to describe how things appear at a casual glance. These would, of course, be vague in Frege's sense.

To reject the induction step of the Sorites argument is to say that it is not in general true that if any member of the series is F, its successor is F also. As we said, this seems to imply that there must be some last member of the series to which the predicate applies. Yet we cannot say which it is. But perhaps if we could explain why we find ourselves in this position of being unable to say where the borderline falls this embarassment might not be an overwhelming difficulty. Possibly the reason why we cannot locate the dividing line is that it is up to us to draw it and there a number of ways of doing so which are equally good. One way of resolving the difficulty, which we have already discussed in section 3.3, is to provide a precise semantic metalanguage for the language containing the vague expressions. The object is to provide a precise meaning or set of alternative precise meanings for each vague expression in the language. An initial worry about such accounts is that if it is admitted that there are in a language expressions whose meanings are vague, it is simply incorrect to assign precise meanings to them. In terms of the dilemma proposed by Dummett and Wright this way out involves ignoring vagueness and is open to their objection that what is ignored is an essential feature of any natural language.

We saw in 3.4 that Fine is aware of this objection and attempts an answer. He suggests that as well as its actual meaning (which determines its definite instances and counter-instances) a predicate has a potential meaning consisting of possibilities for making it precise. For every vague statement there is a range of ways of making all its vague constituents precise. Each way is consistent with potential meanings of the constituents and produces a definite truth value for the whole statement. A statement is definitely true if it is true under every acceptable precisification, definitely false if it is false under every precisification and indeterminate otherwise.

The induction step, as we saw, turns out to be false. For relative to some finite definite set of precisifications of all its vague constituents, a sentence is definitely true, definitely false or indefinite. Then there are exact limits to definite truth. For every precisification there will be some n such that F is true of n but false of its successor. Which it is will vary from one precisification to the next. But provided there is some finite set of precisifications there will be a member of each series which is the last for which it is definitely true that it has the property denoted by F.

The same problem arises however, at a different level in the choice between alternative equally good precise metalanguages. For the choice of any particular set of precisifications would seem to be arbitrary to some extent in that we could always argue for the inclusion of one more way of making some vague expression precise. The vagueness of a vague predicate consists (on the Fregean conception) in exactly this feature: it is unclear just where the limits of the range of possible precise meanings are to be located.

Some have argued that it is wrong to leap from the claim that the induction step is not true to the conclusion that it is therefore false. It does not seem to help much however to say that it is neither true nor false. For the argument can be represented as a chain of particular conditionals and it seems just as implausible to claim of a finely gradated series that at some particular point one of these conditionals ceases to be true as it is to claim that there is a sharp break at some point between true conditionals and false ones. This amounts to saying at some point, in the case of a series of men each of whom has only one more hair than the next, that it is true that one is bald, but neither true nor false that the next is.

One way of trying to make the rejection of the induction step more palatable is to argue that it is only very slightly false. Once it is accepted that the application of vague predicates is a matter of degree the notion of being nearly true or true to any degree may be introduced using some multi-valued logic. A suitable definition of the conditional (such as Machina's, expounded in section 3.3) makes the value of $p \rightarrow q$ less than 1 when p has a higher truth value than q but only just less than 1 when q is almost as true as p. But the problem is that while each conditional (in the chain version of the reasoning) is only just untrue we arrive in the end at outright contradiction. Where there is only a hair's difference between members of a series of balding men and where (n is bald $\rightarrow$ n+1 is bald), (n+1 is bald $\rightarrow$ n+2 is bald) etc. is a chain of conditionals each of which is nearly true, it is not clear how *valid* rules could allow us to arrive at complete falsehoods. The usual answer to this claims that Modus Ponens is not completely valid either. This answer will be discussed in the next section.

It may be pointed out at this point that not all of the conditionals in the chain just mentioned will be less than completely true. For supposing the people at the beginning of the series to be definitely bald, the truth value of the antecedents and consequents of some of the conditionals will be 1 and so the conditionals will be completely true also. And so at some point the truth value of a predication of baldness of a member of the series will have to dip just below 1 despite there being only the difference of a single hair (or less) between that person and the one before. The implausibility of this is hardly less than that of abandoning the induction step as simply false. Wright argues further that the practical notion to be mastered in grasping the meaning of a predicate is that of its application being on balance justified, and since this notion is tolerant, the paradox remains.

The trouble with all the various ways out discussed so far is that they fail to come to terms with the arguments (and intuitions) in favour of the tolerance principles. If, as Dummett and Wright argue, vagueness is to be identified with tolerance and tolerance is an essential feature of the meaning of many expressions of natural language, the induction step cannot be rejected.

5.5 Rejecting the Principles of Classical Logic

Some have suggested that to solve the Paradox we must either abandon some familiar laws and principles of reasoning or hold that an argument, each step of which is valid, may not itself be valid. It has sometimes been suggested that proofs involving predicates of natural language are not to be trusted if they are too long. Short proofs applying principles of logic to natural language do not lead to contradictions. This will not provide a way out of the problems however, for Sorites paradoxes can be generated using quite short series. The sense data theorist's puzzle involving non-transitive indiscernibility of shade may be generated using only three objects.

The main problem with denying the induction step was, as we saw at the beginning of the last section, that its falsehood is taken in classical logic to imply $(\exists n)(Fn \ \& \ -F(n+1))$. So we might try rejecting the move from the negation of $(\forall n)(Fn \rightarrow F(n+1))$ to the conclusion $(\exists n)(Fn \ \& \ -F(n+1))$. This is suggested by Putnam in [2] as being the appropriate response to problems arising because of the undecidability of vague predicates. But it is possible to represent the argument as a series of conditionals. Putnam would then argue that from

$$-(Fx \rightarrow F(x+1))$$

one cannot infer

$$Fx \ \& \ -F(x+1).$$

Instead one should infer

$$--Fx \ \& \ -F(x+1)$$

and reject the move from --Fx to Fx. He claims one can *reject* "John is not bald" without committing oneself to the truth of "John is bald". But this move does not make the rejection of the conditional any more palatable, since it forces us to reject "John is not bald" when John has n hairs and accept "John is not bald" at a time when he has n+1.

Another way out would be to deny that mathematical induction is valid when applied to vague predicates. But, as we saw, the same paradoxical conclusions can be reached using just single steps of Modus Ponens and universal generalization. Even if universal generalization were rejected the unwanted conclusion could be derived for every value of n, though it could not be generalized to conclude that "for every n, if Fn then F(n+1)".

The rejection of Modus Ponens seems an unattractive option. Nevertheless, it is the one suggested recently by several of those working in this area. Chris Peacocke argues in "Are Vague Predicates Coherent?"[44] that it is possible to give an adequate theory of meaning which does not fall foul of Wright's arguments. To preserve the connexion between meaning and understanding the semantics would have to be stated in terms of notions which do not go beyond distinctions manifested in abilities possessed by users of the language. He thinks a coherent semantics can be stated in terms of such notions once it is accepted that vague observational predicates are predicates of degree in his sense. There are degrees to which it is true that something is red, and one thing may deserve the predicate "red" to a greater degree than another. Two objects are red to the same degree on his definition iff *any object not discriminably different from one with respect to colour is not discriminably different in that respect from the other.* Then the degree to which an observational predicate applies to an object is not strictly an observational matter for the two objects may be indiscriminable to an observer yet red to different degrees. The notion is, however, defined in observational terms.

The paradox is avoided in this way, Peacocke claims, for where the conditional

If a is red then b is red

has a consequent with a lower degree of truth than the antecedent we must either say it is false or admit that the use of it in Modus Ponens inferences may fail to preserve truth. The consequent can have a lower degree of truth than the antecedent given the above definition, even though a and b are indiscriminable in shade to all observers. We may retain Modus Ponens, he says, but at the cost of requiring conditionals to be true only when the degree of truth of the consequent is higher than or equal to that of the antecedent. On the other hand, if we decide to accept as true any conditionals involving observational predicates whose antecedent and consequent do not differ discriminably in degree of truth, then we must admit that Modus Ponens is not unrestrictedly valid. The

---

[44] Synthese 46, (1981).

incoherence Wright discovers is due to the attempt to have it both ways: it is not to be blamed on the predicates involved.

Peacocke regards the "if" of the English conditional as vague in that it is not a determinate matter whether or not Modus Ponens is unrestrictedly valid for it or whether it fails to be true where an antecedent has a higher degree of truth than a consequent. But it definitely abandons one or the other property in the presence of vague predicates. However, Wright's arguments for the tolerance of observational predicates might be regarded as forcing us to accept as true conditionals whose antecedent does not differ *very* much from their consequent in degree of truth. The difference in degree of truth may be *detectable* by means of comparisons involving objects apart from those mentioned in antecedent and consequent, but small differences, even where in principle detectable, ought not to make a difference to the applicability of observational predicates. Therefore they ought not to affect the truth values of conditionals of the sort under consideration. It seems that Peacocke is committed to the possibility that at some stage, for some x and y indiscernible from one another with respect to colour, "x is red" is true to degree 1 and "y is red" is true to some degree less than 1. This could only be acceptable if it were possible to view "red" as intolerant to marginal change, that is, as not vague. The point may be put more strongly by switching to Unger's example. On the view being put forward, "It's a swizzle stick", said of some object, may be completely true at one moment and then cease to be completely true at the next when a single atom is removed. For this to be so our concept of a swizzle stick would have to be precise enough to discriminate swizzle sticks from non-swizzle sticks at the atomic level.

Exactly the same kind of problem infects the proposal to reject Modus Ponens. Suppose a conditional involving vague predicates has a consequent whose degree of truth is only very slightly less than the degree of truth of its antecedent, and the antecedent is either completely true or at least true enough to be acceptable in the context of utterance. To refuse to detach the consequent in that context (that is, to refuse to accept it as true or as true enough to be acceptable in the same sense as that in which the antecedent is acceptable) would be to treat the predicates involved as precise.

Peacocke does go some way towards meeting this sort of objection since his notion of degrees of truth is defined in observational terms. There is a problem, however, with the definition he gives of degrees of truth. The trouble is that his notion of degree of truth appears to be inapplicable to observational predicates. For objects which are as red as red roses may be just as red as post-box-red ones. There is a range of shades of red which things may have and still truly be said to be red, that is, to be red to degree 1. If this is so there is no difference in the degree to which they are red. But on Peacocke's definition they cannot be red to the same degree, since many objects indiscernible with respect to colour from one will differ discernibly in colour from others. It is not because of vagueness (in the second sense he mentions in part III) that there is no total ordering of observable properties: this difficulty applies to all other observational predicates and there appears to be no simple way out.

5.6 Austerity Measures

The incoherence thesis should be of particular interest to semantic theorists and some have replied to the challenge Wright's arguments present. In the introduction to their book *Truth and Meaning*, Evans and McDowell argue that Wright's conclusions demonstrate the futility of a certain kind of approach to semantic theory. The approach they think should be rejected is one which attempts by means of conceptual breakdown to account for meaning relations (entailments for example) between statements. In the more austere homophonic truth theory which they prefer the meaning of each sentence is to be given by using that sentence to state its own truth conditions. The meanings of significant expressions generally is given in this way by rules such as

Something satisfies "is red" iff it is red.

They write:[45]

> A semantic description of a language in this style, dealing with vague predicates by using those very predicates, would be systematic without being vulnerable to Wright's accusations ..... of incoherence. Wright's paper is in fact a valuable attack on the underpinnings of the view that semantics must effect conceptual breakdown.

The moral they draw from Wright's argument is that we must rest content with their austere variety of meaning theory.

---

[45] Evans and McDowell [1], p.xi.

Wright disagrees with this moral. In his "Rule Following, Objectivity and The Theory of Meaning" he argues against the claim of truth theory to provide an adequate theory of meaning for natural language. Since his reasons are not closely connected with vagueness we need not investigate them here. But the Evans-McDowell response clearly fails to dispose of the paradox. To point out that the difficulties discussed in the last chapter cannot be generated within the austere truth theory preferred by the authors does not throw much light on either problem. Again, no reason has been given for rejecting tolerance rules: no suggestion has been made that they are false or not involved in the meanings (in some appropriate sense) of vague predicates. We are simply told that such meaning relations are not to be incorporated into semantic theory. This does not touch the paradox. Furthermore, if Sorites arguments can be used to show that ordinary predicates are incoherent then those predicates cannot be used in truth theory in the way Evans and McDowell propose: to express truth conditions for a vague language. The theory which made use of them would contain incoherent elements, even if the incoherence could not be demonstrated within the resources of that theory.

5.7 Paradigm Exemplars and Knowledge of Tolerance Rules

In *Ways of Meaning*, chapter IX, Mark Platts, attempts to provide some further argument for Evans and McDowell's response. He recognizes some of the above objections and admits the need for an argument against the non-decompositional analysis apart from the *ad hoc* need to avoid the paradox. He first suggests a solution to a novel version of the paradox and attempts to generalize it. The version he devises involves an arrangement of black dots on a white surface which constitute a picture of a face. The appropriate tolerance rule would have us accept

> If a certain arrangement of dots is a picture of a face, so is the same arrangement with one dot slightly moved or removed

But then (by now familiar reasoning) it would follow that all arrangements of black dots on white would be pictures of a face. Platts objects that this conditional premiss cannot be deduced from rules of sense for the predicate, rules which, it could plausibly be argued, must be known by users of the language. For such rules would have to relate the application conditions of "is a picture of a face" to the application conditions of predicates concerning pure dot arrangements. Obviously, someone could recognize a picture of a face (in a newspaper, for example) whilst knowing nothing of pure dot arrangements. Mastery of the former sort of predicate is not grounded in mastery of the latter, and any rules relating the two would falsify our understanding. Similarly, competence in the application of the predicate "heap" does not depend upon mastery of numerical predicates concerning numbers of grains.

Platts admits that this argument is difficult to generalize to other cases. Tolerance rules for colour predicates are stated just in terms of indiscernibility with respect to colour and it does seem that anyone who understood such a predicate would have to be credited with grasping such rules (in some sense). And it seems that tolerance rules for other predicates such as "heap" and "is a picture of a face" could be stated (rather vaguely) in terms of indiscernibility without any mention of precise quantities or other notions which might be unknown to speakers.[46]

If tolerance rules do express truths about the application conditions of vague predicates the paradox is still with us. As we saw in the last section, it does not seem to help to argue that the rules should not be incorporated into the semantic theory for the language. Platts makes another attempt to dissolve the paradox which might be used against tolerance rules stated vaguely, just in terms of indiscernibility. He argues that we grasp the use of observational predicates in part through exposure to paradigm exemplars. Perceived similarities and dissimilarities to these determine further applications of the predicate, and our grasp of these further applications continues to operate in some way after the paradigms are forgotten. He points out that indiscernibility from a paradigm does not make something a paradigm, though it does determine the application to it of the appropriate predicate. Indiscriminability from a paradigm is an observationally

---

[46] Alternatively, it might be argued that though Wright does argue for the view that tolerance is part of the sense of observational predicates, it might be better to take his arguments as establishing that the tolerance of such predicates is a consequence of facts about their sense or facts about the conditions in which they are standardly employed. On this view tolerance rules are not part of what is known by competent users of observational predicates but are a consequence of features of such predicates' use and their truth could still be used as support for the induction step.

determinable sufficient condition for the application of a vague predicate.

The trouble with this argument is that it does not seem to stop us from arguing that there may be other sufficient conditions for the application of observational predicates: those stated in tolerance rules, for example. There appears to be no inconsistency between accepting these as well as Platts remarks about paradigms. Platts seems to think there is some tension here in that the role of indiscriminability in determining the truth of observational predicates should be characterized in terms of paradigms but no argument is presented as to why this is so. This suggestion does, however, provide a valuable clue to the solution to the Paradox to be developed in the next chapter.

5.8 Vagueness and Contextual Disambiguation

In "The Paradox of the Heap" Hans Kamp [2] suggests a novel solution to the Sorites which attempts to accommodate Wright's arguments for tolerance whilst avoiding his pessimistic conclusions about the prospects for providing coherent semantic theories for vague languages. Kamp rejects his own previous supervaluation account (Kamp [1]) for reasons similar to those advanced in 5.4: the rejection of the induction step is taken in classical logic to imply that there is some last member of the Sorites series to which the vague predicate applies - a value of n such that P(n) & -P(n+1). Not only is there no non-arbitrary value of n for which this is true, but as Dummett and Wright show, to suppose that there is conflicts with the observationality of many vague predicates. There can be no sharp limits to the scope of application of predicates governed by the principle that both of a pair of observationally indistinguishable objects deserve such a predicate if either does.

To this sort of objection supervaluation theorists may respond by agreeing that though no single determinate extension is fixed by the meaning of a vague predicate, there may be a number of equally good boundary points corresponding to alternative construals of the positive and negative extensions and the truth value gap of the predicate. What is needed then is the notion of a collection of models and the sort of semantics investigated in 3.4. But as Kamp points out the choice of one particular set of models rather than another is also arbitrary, since nothing about the semantics of natural language predicates determines the exclusion of certain other models specifying more or less generous boundaries to the extensions of various predicates.

Kamp's solution to the Sorites, in [2], involves maintaining that the the induction step is false but, like Putnam, he rejects the claim that $(\exists n)(P(n)\ \&\ -P(n+1))$ must therefore be true. He also accepts the validity of MPP and the truth of the individual conditionals $(P(i) \rightarrow P(i+1))$, $(P(i+1) \rightarrow P(i+2))$ etc. on the grounds of Dummett's and Wright's arguments for tolerance. So universal generalization fails also. This option was mentioned and rejected above (in 5.4) on the grounds that paradoxical conclusions can still be derived using just the particular conditionals and MPP. The conclusion P(n) can still be derived for each value of n, even though the general conclusion $(\forall n)(P(n) \rightarrow P(n+1))$ cannot be drawn. However, Kamp's account contains further complications designed to out-manoeuvre this reply.[47]

First, his diagnosis of the paradox. As mentioned above, he accepts tolerance rules as part of the logic of vague observational predicates. An object falls within the positive extension of such a predicate, he claims, when it is indistinguishable in respects relevant to the predicate's application from an object already accepted as belonging within its positive extension.[48] Which objects these are is, he thinks, a matter to be determined largely by context in the case of vague predicates such as "heavy" or "clever". Context supplies participants in a conversation with background information which can resolve otherwise undecidable questions concerning the predicate's application to certain objects. In the context of presentation of a Sorites series there are objects available at the far ends of the series with which the dubious cases towards the middle may be compared. So as well as the tendency to say on the basis of tolerance rules that each object deserves the predicate applied at the previous stage to its observationally indistinguishable neighbour, there is a growing

47 It is not clear why Kamp rejects the induction step of the Sorites argument but accepts, on the grounds of the arguments for tolerance, the particular conditionals of the chain version mentioned above. The arguments for tolerance clearly offer as much support for the general claim that a natural language predicate which applies to one member of a suitable gradated series must always apply to the next member as they do for each particular conditional concerning individual members of such a series. If observationally indiscernible objects must get the same observational predicates then the induction step is surely true.

48 Kamp calls this principle EOI: equivalence of observationally indistinguishable objects. We shall continue to use Wright's terminology, since there is no important difference between the two notions.

tendency as the series is surveyed to refuse to apply the predicate to some members of the series on the grounds that they resemble too closely things at the far end which clearly do not deserve the predicate. The ends of the series serve as "anchor points" whose resemblance to intermediate objects must be balanced against the pull of tolerance principles. There is also a less strong tendency in the situation in which observationally indistinguishable pairs of objects are seen in isolation from the end points for the judgement of each object on its own merits to eventually outweigh the commitment to tolerance.

Either way we will inevitably call a halt somewhere to the application of the predicate. Kamp points out that this account of the situation agrees with Wright's in that it takes us to be in the grip of conflicting tendencies and so assumes some incoherence in the underlying semantic principles.[49]

The important feature of contexts for developing this insight into the paradox is the body of background information they contain. This is understood to consist of (at least) the set of statements accepted by the participants in the discourse taking place in the context. It also contains all those statements involving an application of the vague predicate in uncontroversial cases, that is, the statements which would be accepted as true (or as false) in any context. In other controversial cases context can determine truth value. But the addition of new statements also affects context. At each stage of the Sorites reasoning further applications of the predicate to objects are added to the general store of background information producing at each stage a new context. At some point the addition of a further statement will have to be judged not coherently incorporable: its addition would create an incoherent context since it would explicitly or implicitly clash with statements already accepted.

The notion of a *context sensitive model* is needed to develop this solution to the paradox. Where L_o is language containing the usual vocabulary, including variables, constants and just one one-place predicate, P, an appropriate general context sensitive model will be an 8-tuple <U, F, C, Coh, Inc, B, m, ~> such that U is the universe of discourse, F a function assigning elements of U to each individual constant of L_o and a pair of disjunct subsets

---

[49] Neither Kamp nor Wright says what is conflicting with tolerance. It is worth noting here, in anticipation of the account to be argued in chapter 6, that Kamp's clearer analysis of the situation makes it evident that it is tolerance that is pulling in *both* directions.

of U to each predicate letter P (the positive and negative extension of P denoted as $F^{+}(P)$ and $F^{-}(P)$ respectively), C is the non-empty set of contexts, Coh and Inc disjoint subsets of C (the set of coherent and incoherent contexts), B a function assigning sets of background statements to contexts, m a function which modifies contexts by incorporating sets of statements into them, and ~ a binary relation which holds between objects in U when they are observationally indiscernible from one another. General context sensitive models must meet the following two conditions:

(1) $B(c) \subseteq B(m(c,\Gamma))$ and $\Gamma \subseteq B(m(c,\Gamma))$

(2) if $\Gamma \subseteq B(c)$ then $m(c,\Gamma) = c$.

Assuming $\vdash$ is a suitable entailment relation, a context sensitive model relative to $\vdash$ will be a general context sensitive model as just defined which meets the three further requirements:

(a) If for some ϕ which is a member of the set of sentences of L_O $B(c) \vdash \phi$ and $B(c) \vdash -\phi$ then $c \in$ Inc

(b) for each $C \in Coh_M$, B(c) is closed under $\vdash$ (any statements entailed by members of the background of c are also members of the background of c)

(c) each member of the set C contains as part of its background the positive and negative extension of P (the union of the sets $F_M{}^{+}(P)$ and $F_M{}^{-}(P)$, which is referred to as the set D_M).

Truth conditions for atomic statements, conditionals, conjunctions, disjunctions and quantified statements will contain complexities due to the context dependence of the truth of statements of these sorts. Where $[\phi]_{M,c}$ is read as the "the truth value of ϕ in model M and context $c \in C_M$ relative to the entailment relation $\vdash$", the truth conditions for atomic, conditional and quantified statements are as follows:

(i) $[P(c_i)]^{\vdash}_{M,c} = 1$ iff $(\exists b \in U_M)(b \sim F_M(c_i)$ & $P(\bar{b}) \in B_M(c))$

(ii) $[P(c_i)]^{\vdash}_{M,c} = 0$ iff $(\exists b \in U_M)(b \sim F_M(c_i)$ & $-P(\bar{b}) \in B_M(c))$

(iii) $[\phi \rightarrow \psi]^{\vdash}_{M,c} = 1$ iff $[\phi]^{\vdash}_{M,c} = O$ or $[\psi]^{\vdash}_{M,m(c,\phi)} = 1$

(iv) $[\phi \rightarrow \psi]^{\vdash}_{M,c} = O$ iff $[\phi]^{\vdash}_{M,c} = 1$ and $[\psi]^{\vdash}_{M,m(c,\phi)} = O$

(v) $[(\forall v_i)\phi]^{\vdash}_{M,c} = 1$ iff $m_M(c,(\forall v_i)\phi) \in Coh_M$

$\&(\forall a \in U_M)[\phi^{\bar{a}}{}_{\bar{v}i}]^{\vdash}_{M,c} = 1$

(vi) $[(\forall v_i)\phi]^{\vdash}_{M,c} = O$ iff $m_M(c,(\forall v_i)\phi) \in Inc_M$ or $(\exists a$

$\in U_M)[\phi^{\bar{a}}{}_{\bar{v}i}]^{\vdash}_{M,c} = O$

(vii) $[(\exists v_i)\phi(v_i)]^{\vdash}_{M,c} = 1$ iff for some $a \in U_M$ $[\phi(a)]^{\vdash}_{M,c} = 1$

(viii) $[(\exists v_i)\phi(v_i)]^{\vdash}_{M,c} = O$ iff for every $a \in U_M[\phi(a)]^{\vdash}_{M,c} = O$

So the universal statement $(\forall n)(P(n) \rightarrow P(n+1))$ will be false since its addition to a coherent context produces incoherence. But $(\exists n)(P(n)$ & $-P(n+1))$ will be false also in such contexts: there is no value of n for which it is true, since each conditional of the form $P(a) \rightarrow P(a+1)$ is true. Each particular conditional may be true without the universal generalization being true in any context.

The "chain" version of the Sorites, involving just a string of particular conditionals, is supposed to be blocked in the following way. The idea is that starting with a coherent context and adding more and more statements we can end up with a context which involves inconsistent commitments. Suppose the statement P(k) is accepted and true in a coherent context c, and suppose k~k+1. The conditional P(k) → P(k+1) is also true in such a context because of tolerance (Kamp's EOI).

$$[P(k) \rightarrow P(k+1)]_c = 1 \quad \text{if} \quad [P(k+1)]_{m(c,Pk)} = 1$$

But although P(k) and (P(k) → P(k+1)) are both true in c, the truth of P(k+1) in c may not be derivable. This is because the addition of (P(k) → P(k+1)) to the background of c may create an incoherent context. Though c is coherent m(c,(P(k) → P(k+1))) is not, and nothing can be validly inferred from the premisses which constitute the background of an inconsistent context. The definition of validity which Kamp prefers is as follows:

> For any subset Γ of the sentences of L_O and sentence φ of L_O, φ *can be validly inferred from Γ* if for every context sensitive model M relative to ⊢, and every c ∈ C_M, if m(c,Γ) is sound then $[\phi]_{M,m(c,\Gamma)} = 1$.

(A sound context is one which is coherent and whose background statements are all true.) So we cannot use the truth of P(k) and P(k) → P(k+1) at c to force the application of the predicate further through the series.

Kamp is here imposing something like the requirement of total evidence on the concept of deductive validity. No matter how strong an inductive argument seems to be on its own merits, its conclusion cannot safely be detached and added to our store of knowledge if it conflicts with other parts of that knowledge. Kamp's notion of valid inference forces us to take other relevant contextually available information into account in deductive inference also. There might appear to be a significant disanalogy here in that Kamp requires the premisses of the potential inference to be compatible with other background knowledge, and in the inductive case it is the conclusion which must be checked for consistency with other relevant information. But it is clear from his remarks about the conditions for contextual consistency that the potential for generating a further statement incompatible with some background information is sufficient to render one set of statements incompatible with that background information.

Though this seems at first sight to be the most promising attempt so far to accommodate Wright's arguments for tolerance without being forced to his conclusions, it does not manage to avoid the paradoxical conclusions of the Sorites in the chain version unless some *ad hoc* constraints are built into his notion of entailment. For consider the following argument: we assume

(i) c is some sound context (in the above sense)

(ii) $B(c) \vdash P(k)$

and (iii) k~k+1 as before.

(iv) $(P(k) \rightarrow P(k+1))$ will be true at c (since each such conditional will be true at c by EOI),

and by the truth conditions for "→" it follows that

(v) P(k+1) must be true at the context m(c,P(k)). (For P(k) is true at c.)

But (vi) m(c,P(k)) = c (by condition (2) of the definition of a general context sensitive model given above).

So (vii) P(k+1) will therefore be true at the context c.

Also (viii) $P(k+1) \vdash B(c)$ (by condition (b) on a context senstive model, as above).

It can be established in the same way that P(k+2) is true at c and also P(k+3) and so on. Since each conditional $(P(k+n) \rightarrow P(k+n+1))$ is true at c, the truth of its consequent can be shown to be true at that context. So there is no stopping the indiscriminate spread of vague predicates. The important point about this proof is that MPP is *not* required to establish the conclusion. (viii) follows just from the argument (i) - (vii) above, which merely employs Kamp's definitions and truth conditions for '→' in a straightforword fashion. To block the conclusion that the consequent of each of the string of conditionals is contained in the background of context c, he would have to employ a notion of entailment which rejected some step in this argument ((i)-(viii)), and such a conception would surely have to deviate from the one we standardly use. So his restrictions on what may be inferred in coherent contexts fails to stop the drift. The Sorites Paradox is not solved.[51]

[51] It is not clear what the difference between being true at a context and being incorporated into the background of a context really comes to. At

inferred in coherent contexts fails to stop the drift. The Sorites Paradox is not solved.[50]

Once tolerance principles are built into the truth conditions of atomic sentences, it is hard to see how widespread incoherence is to be avoided. Any context can be proved incoherent so long as there is a statement [P(a)] true in that context and objects b and d such that a~b and b~d but not a~d, and [P(d)] is false in the context. In the postscript to the article Kamp outlines a version of this difficulty. Sentences can come out both true and false in the same coherent context. This seems to be a lesser problem than the one above, for minor incoherences might be expected to occur in actual contexts involving natural language predicates. As Kamp remarks[51] in conclusion,

> "The sentences which are liable to get both truth values in coherent contexts are, as far as I can see, always sentences about the truth values of which we have no very clear intuitions anyway, and the fact that such a sentence may end up with both truth values might even be interpreted as an indication of why our intuitions about such sentences are uncertain or confused".

But if the Sorites argument cannot be blocked we will be forced to admit as true in any coherent context the application of a vague predicate to any object whatsoever. Sentences which seem to our intuitions to be clearly false will end up true and vice versa. It is this more serious difficulty which makes Kamp's account unsatisfactory.

In chapter 9 we shall suggest a way out of the underlying problem of reconciling model theoretic approaches to the semantics of vague natural languages with the tolerance of the predicates contained in those languages and also develop a rather more straightforward account of the context-dependency of vague predicates.

---

50 It is not clear what the difference between being true at a context and being incorporated into the background of a context really comes to. At any rate the challenge presented by Wright and Dummett is just to show how to prevent the conclusions of the Sorites turning out to be true in a context - any context - and that challenge does not seem to have been met here.

51 Kamp [2], p.275.

Chapter 6

A SOLUTION TO THE PARADOX

6.1 Tolerance Principles and Pure Observationality

It appears to be as difficult to argue against the incoherence thesis which emerges from Wright's and Dummett's arguments as it is to accept it. For if we try to argue against any premiss on the grounds that it leads to obviously false or contradictory conclusions, there is always the reply available that this is further evidence of deeply embedded inconsistency in this part of the language.[53]

It is possible, however, to take the arguments of 4.2 as establishing not only that there are no purely phenomenal properties (Dummett's conclusion), but also as showing that there is no purely observational language. If there were it would be massively incoherent, and we have good evidence that this is not so. We will now turn back to Wright's arguments for the incoherence thesis.

One of these arguments made use of the premiss that there are purely observational predicates: ones whose application may be determined solely by the use of the senses whenever it may be determined at all. Wright argued that these at least must be tolerant, since no other considerations could be allowed to undermine judgements about their application made by competent observers. Where one of a pair of things observers cannot tell apart deserves a purely observational predicate, the other must deserve it also. But a language containing tolerant predicates must

---

[53] It might be argued that the problem only appears to be this intractable from Dummett's and Wright's antiholist perspective on the nature of language. A holist must, of course, reject the incoherence thesis having staked so much on the overall consistency and coherence of the rules and concepts which determine the use of the language. We shall not pursue this line of attack on Dummett and Wright directly, as it is unclear what variety of holism would provide a route out of the argument or how it should be developed. It is even less clear what bearing the adoption of such a view of language would have on their views on the paradox. But see the remarks in 6.2 and 6.3 on conceptual holism.

be radically incoherent, since those predicates ought to apply indiscriminately.

Wright's reasoning provides us with a *reductio* of the notion of pure observationality. The argument goes as follows. Suppose there were some purely observational predicates. They would by definition apply to things just on the basis of the way those things appeared to casual observers. Nothing else could undermine the judgement of a normal observer that such a predicate applied. Therefore they would be tolerant. But when applied consistently they would lead to conclusions which *conflicted* with the judgements of those observers. (The tolerance rule for the predicate "red" would lead for instance to the conclusion that grass is red). If a predicate really is tolerant it must apply in cases where simple observation tells us it does not apply. To apply it in these cases would be to override the judgements of competent observers. So if a predicate is purely observational it is tolerant, and if it is tolerant it cannot be purely observational. Therefore there can be no purely observational predicates; if there were, they would be tolerant, and if they were tolerant they would not be purely observational.

A *reductio* argument designed to undermine the incoherence thesis might look to be in danger of providing further evidence for that thesis. Can the incoherence thesis simply absorb this argument as further grist for its mill? I think not, for it attacks a premiss of one of the arguments for the thesis. The incoherence must be located in the view assumed by Dummett and Wright: that language has a distinct, purely observational part.

Dummett's and Wright's arguments might therefore be taken as establishing that there is no part of the language whose use is determined just by direct observation of the world without any admixture of theory. We shall see in the following sections that further considerations of a similar kind to this are sufficient to resolve the Sorites Paradox and demolish the incoherence thesis.[54]

---

[54] It will emerge later (in chapters 6, 7 and 8) that there are problems with the above *reductio* argument against pure observationality. There are however other well known grounds for doubting Wright's assumption of a sharp distinction between observation and theory. See Suppe [1] for a summary of some of the literature on this topic. We shall not pursue the various other lines of attack on the distinction since it is not clear what bearing they have on our main problem: establishing the coherence of natural language. We shall assume that it makes sense to suppose some parts of the language are more observational than others, and in the next

6.2 Counter-examples to Tolerance Principles

Wright's other arguments for the tolerance rules, the arguments about learnability and the limitations of our senses and memories, do not rely on the assumption that there are any purely observational predicates. They are meant to apply to all highly observational predicates: those usually or standardly applied on the basis of appearance. The point of these arguments is to establish that two things could not appear the same to casual observers and yet one but not the other deserve one of these predicates. But as we know, appearances may be deceptive: two things may be indistinguishable to casual observers and yet one but not the other deserve some observational predicate. Illusions and tricks of the light may make someone who is not bald look just as hairless as a genuinely bald person; one heap may look as large as another when the two are seen from a certain angle and distance and yet the second may turn out to be much smaller and perhaps not a heap at all. The strict tolerance rules for which Wright argues do not seem generally to be true.

Differences that could not be detected at a glance may make a difference to the applicability of the predicate "child". Suppose a twenty-year-old dwarf was so like his twelve-year-old nephew in appearance that they were always taken to be identical twins. One but not the other would be a child. Another example shows the predicate may not be tolerant with respect to numbers of heart beats. Normally, someone does not cease to be a child between one heart beat and the next. A case could be imagined however, where a child's heart stopped beating but its owner was kept alive and remained in a coma for several years until a suitable heart transplant was found. Suppose the child's physical development was normal in this time. When revived, at their next heart beat they might be a child no longer.

So, wherever a predicate is determined by a number of concepts which can vary independently there will be counter-examples to the tolerance rule for that predicate. There could be a series which varied continuously with respect to the concept ϕ but where a predicate determined by this concept was true of some member but clearly not true of the next. No matter how smoothly the series varied with respect to one determining concept there

---

section will consider Wright's and Dummett's arguments as they apply to highly observational predicates.

could be large differences with respect to another, differences which would justify the drawing of sharp boundaries.

Another example concerns the predicate "heap". Where one thing in a smoothly varying series is a heap the next may not be, even though it contains only one less grain. For the concept of shape determines the predicate "heap" as well as the concept of number of grains. If one member of a series consists of many grains "heaped up" in a single mass and the next almost the same number raked out flat, the first will be a heap and the second not. Nor does shape alone determine the predicate for, in terms of shape alone, a pinch might be indiscernible from a genuine heap. And a hollow stage set might be indiscernible in terms of both shape and size from a real heap.

We could also imagine circumstances in which one man is bald but a second with only one more hair is not. Suppose the first, genuinely bald man has no hairs at all on the top of his head but quite a few around the sides and back. The second has only one more hair but has had a cunning hair transplant and his hairs are now distributed evenly over the top of his scalp. He is happily non-bald despite having only one more hair than someone clearly bald.

The evidence both from psychology and ordinary introspection is in favour of the view that appearances are complex and have a structure, even in the most apparently simple cases. And so it seems there will always be a multiplicity of factors determining the application of any observational predicate. A concept does not determine the application of a predicate in isolation from other concepts. Let us call this view "conceptual holism" to distinguish it from other epistemic and semantic varieties of holism.

6.3 A Reply, and a Review of the Nature of the Sorites Series

These counter-examples to the tolerance rules produced by the multiplicity of determining concepts may seem to create no more than a trifling difficulty for Wright's arguments. It is a mere problem, surely, about formulating the tolerance rules in the right way. For these arguments apply to situations where there is no detectable variation in any respect relevant to the application of a predicate, and these counter-examples seem to miss his main point since they involve sudden alterations in particular respects. A natural way of dealing with this problem would be to revise the conception of the series which involve the induction step. Surely the induction step should be understood as applying just to series whose members vary continuously only with respect to some one determining concept *all others remaining fixed.* It seems that when we imagine the series we do think of it in just this way: as varying smoothly in a single dimension, all other variables remaining constant. But although we vaguely think we can imagine such series, it seems that there cannot be any in nature, that is, if conceptual holism is correct. Members of a series could not vary just with respect to one determining concept while remaining fixed in all others, for concepts do not according to the holist operate in isolation in this way.

The conceptual holist is surely right about this. What we vaguely think we imagine could not be the case. For no actual series could give the impression of continuous variation with respect to colour, for instance, without varying also with respect to some particular determinate colour or colours. And if the series looks more orange as it is scanned from left to right, then it will also look less red. A series of heaps cannot vary just with respect to the number of grains its members contain: if they vary in this way they must vary with respect to size also. And a person could not change with respect to apparent maturity without also altering in more particular respects.

What is really needed to eliminate these counter-examples is the notion of a series which varies with respect to some group of interdependent determining concepts. It will have to do so in such a way that no difference between one member and the next with respect to any of these could be discerned on a casual inspection. And the series will either have to vary not at all with respect to other determining concepts independent of those in this group, or else not vary noticeably with respect to any of them. Concepts are interdependent, let's say, when either there are lawlike connexions between them (so a change with respect to one inevitably brings about or is brought about by a change with respect to the other), or one is supervenient[55] upon the other in some situation.

6.4 Revising Tolerance Rules

The tolerance principles which support the induction step must also be revised to protect them from these counter-examples. Strict tolerance rules must be replaced by principles of the following kind:

---

[55] Differences in apparent maturity will, for example, supervene upon more particular differences, though there may be no direct lawlike connexions.

If one thing is a heap and a second differs from it in containing only one less grain and in any other ways dependent on this minor difference but the two do not differ detectably in any other respects relevant to the application of the predicate "heap", then the second is a heap also.

If one person is a child and a second differs from the first only marginally in appearance with respect to physical maturity and in whatever other respects are dependent on this but there are no other differences between them relevant to the applicability of the predicate "child", then the second is a child also.

Principles of this loose sort differ from the strict versions of tolerance rules in containing an exception clause. Perhaps we read the strict version of the rules as implicitly containing such a clause. The antecedents of natural language conditionals are often read as containing an implicit supposition that other things are to remain the same, that, apart from the change introduced explicitly by the antecedent, there is no relevant variation.

There are good reasons for supposing that it would not be possible to make these rules more precise. For to spell out exhaustively the *ceteris paribus* clause it would be necessary to determine all the respects which might count, in advance of all imaginable and unimaginable circumstances, as relevant to the application of the predicate. If observational predicates do have open texture, as is suggested by Waismann in [1] and others, following Wittgenstein, this task would not be possible. As we saw in section 1.6 the existence of open texture means that we do not have precise rules available to determine a predicate's application in all possible circumstances. So loose rules cannot be made more precise.

We can, however, specify in a general way when some respect is relevant to the application of a predicate. For suppose some object differs from others to which a predicate applies in possessing (or not possessing) some particular property and those others which are within the scope of the predicate would not have been so had they possessed (or not possessed) this property. Knowing this we would not be inclined to extend the predicate to the new case as it differs significantly from others to which the predicate certainly does apply. So assuming that there is a further predicate available to describe this difference, we may state the general schema for the appropriate tolerance rules as follows:

> ***If two things, a and b, are indistinguishable with respect to some group of interdependent concepts, C, which are all determining concepts for the predicate F and F applies to a, then F applies to b also unless there is some other predicate, H, which applies to a but not to b and which is such that if a had not been H it would not have been F.***

Lack of H (which may be a negative characteristic) means that b cannot safely be included in the scope of the predicate F. Where F is the predicate "heap" and ϕ the concept of quantity of grains, H might be a predicate of shape (such as being conical). Or, where ϕ is some concept to do with a person's superficial appearance in respect of maturity, and F the predicate "child", H might be the predicate "is over twelve years of age".

When tolerance rules are understood in this loose way they are surely true. Minor differences between things which would go unnoticed in the circumstances in which a predicate is normally applied cannot matter for its application once all other relevant variation is excluded. If an observational predicate applies to the one, it must also apply to the other when we cannot by observation discover any relevant difference between them. But now doubts begin to arise about the existence of such series, doubts about the assumption on which the Sorites argument rests. Is it possible to find a series which meets the complex conditions we have seen to be necessary? The argument that it is not occupies the next section.

6.5 A Way Out of the Paradox

A suitable series would have to be such that a predicate F applied at one end but not the other where F is an observational predicate. We saw that the actual variation throughout this series would be with respect to some group of interdependent determining concepts, and it would have to be so gradual that no noticeable difference could be discerned by mere observation from member to member with respect to any concept in this set. Let us call the set C. Obviously, indiscernibility has to behave non-transitively somewhere in the series or F could not be true at one end and not at the other. Suppose some concept ϕ is a member of C. Each member is, we shall assume, indiscernible from the next with respect to ϕ. Now, consider the concept of a pair of things being *indiscernible to some observer with respect to ϕ*. This concept will have to be a member of the set C also. For these two concepts, of ϕ and of indiscernibility with respect to ϕ, are interrelated in lawlike ways. If the colour of a thing changes this will alter its indiscernibility from other things with respect to colour and vice versa. So where ϕ is a member of a set of determining concepts for a predicate F, indiscernibility with respect to ϕ will be also.

But now we will find that at some point in the series there is a relevant difference in a determining respect from one member to the next. Let o be an observer of a series, and let S_1 and S_n be the end members of the series or of any portion of the series sufficiently long for S_1 and S_n to be discernibly different with respect to ϕ. Each member is indiscernible to o from the next member in this respect. But, if the end members are to be discernibly different in this way indiscernibility relations must behave non-transitively somewhere along the series. So, for any series or portion of a series, there must be adjacent members, S_i and S_{i-1}, such that

(i) S_i is indiscernible with respect to ϕ from S_{i-1} to observer o

(ii) S_{i-1} is indiscernible with respect to ϕ from S_1 to o

(iii) S_i is just discernibly different with respect to ϕ from S_1 to o.

Thus S_i and S_{i-1} are just discernibly different with respect to indiscernibility from S_1 with respect to ϕ. Since this concept is a member of C, there will be a difference in a determining respect between adjacent members of any suitable series. But where there is an observable difference between some neighbouring pair in a respect relevant to the application of some observational predicate, then that predicate may quite consistently be applied to one of the pair but not the other.

It does not seem difficult to find an apparently straightforward proof of (i)-(iii). S_n can be discerned by an observer o to be different from S_1 with respect to ϕ. If no earlier member of the series (or subseries) has this property, so that S_n is the first, then

S_n is S_i and S_{i-1} is S_{n-1}. If some member of the series earlier than S_n is seen by o to be different from S_1 with respect to ϕ there must be a first such member. If there were not, none of the members could have this property and we know some have it. Since there must be a first member in any finite series to have any property which some members of that series have, there will always be a first member to have the property of appearing to o to be discernibly different from S_1 with respect to ϕ. This member is S_i. Since it is the first, S_{i-1} is not discernible from S_1 with respect to ϕ. So we have shown that there must be adjacent members of the series (or subseries) which differ with respect to a determining concept for F.

The same argument might be used to show that for any observer there will be a pair of adjacent members, S_j and S_{j-1}, which are indiscernible from each other to that observer and which are such that S_j is also indiscernible for that observer from S_n (the last member of the series or subseries) while S_{j-1} is just discernibly different from S_n. Which pair of adjacent members this is will, of course, vary from observer to observer.

It is likely that this proof of (i)-(iii) would be rejected by many of those impressed by Dummett's and Wright's arguments. They would argue that it depends on the principle, rendered dubious by the existence of vague predicates, that there must always be a first member of a series to have a property possessed by some members of the series. It is precisely this principle which is in dispute when it is claimed predicates can be vague in Frege's sense of having no sharp boundaries to their scope. However, indiscernibility from the end members of a series cannot be vague in this Fregean sense. For it cannot be a transitive relation: indiscernibility of one object from an end member of a series in which it is embedded is no guarantee that that object's immediate neighbour will also be indiscernible from the same end member. Dummett points out (in [1], p.320) that the kind of paradoxical conclusions he is discussing arise for observational predicates only. There is no reason, he says, to suppose relational expressions are vague in the same way as observational predicates. "Discriminibly different" and "indiscriminable from" are obviously relational. Indeed, he says we must take observational relational expressions such as "indiscernible from" and "discriminably different from" as being governed by consistent rules of use and completely definite.

Thus we may rely upon the commonsense argument that an observer who sees that the end members of a series look different from one another in some respect and judges the first few members to be indiscernible from the initial member cannot go on judging all the succeeding members to be indiscernible from that initial member. They must start noticing a difference from an end member somewhere. The conclusion must be that the predicate "indiscernible to o with respect to ϕ" must be sharply bounded. Such predicates are not tolerant. And so we may in this context accept the principle that in any ordered series there must be a first member to deserve a predicate deserved by some members. For the principle is only dubious where predicates are vague in ways which render them tolerant. Possible objections to this will be discussed in the next chapter.

Granting (i)-(iii), it may be felt that some further argument is required to establish the *relevance* to the predicate F of the relational property of indiscernibility for o with respect to ϕ. For, despite the argument three paragraphs back that where ϕ is a member of C indiscernibility for o with respect to ϕ must be also, it could be thought that it is just how a thing looks with respect to colour which determines whether or not the predicate "red" applies to it, not its relation to other things.

The further arguments for the inclusion of these indiscernibilities as relevant to the application of a predicate are just those arguments Wright gives for tolerance. These are arguments we have accepted, though we claimed that they establish loose tolerance rules rather than Wright's strict ones. For the arguments for tolerance are meant to show that comparisons with other objects determine the application of an observational predicate - things that appear the same must get all the same observational predicates. On the strict principles, indiscernibilities between pairs of objects in respects relevant to the application of a predicate force the application of that predicate to both objects or to neither. If this is so, those indiscernibilities are relevant to the application of the predicate. The plausibility of this has not been denied. All that is being claimed here is that tolerance rules must be understood as loose rules, and when they are the paradox disappears. Anything y indiscernible from a red thing x is red also provided there are no other relevant differences; there is a relevant difference when one but not the other differs in colour from some third thing z. If the first indiscernibility (between x and y) is relevant to the projection of the predicate from x to y, so is the indiscernibility between y and z.

Let us first see how this might work in a particular case and then, in the next section, consider some objections to the general strategy used above. Suppose S_j is some strip towards the middle of the colour series, and an observer has judged that all the previously examined strips, up to and including S_{j-1}, to be red. Now, that observer notices that S_j has a property that all these previously examined ones lacked: it is indiscernible in colour from a further strip, S_n, which looks orange. Since S_j is indiscernible both from this one and from one the observer had decided to call red, they may decide that S_j is a borderline case and so deserving of neither predicate.

Alternatively, S_j might appear indiscernible in colour from something which is clearly a borderline case deserving neither the predicate "red" nor the predicate "orange". Is the observer forced to say that S_j is a borderline case also? Or are they forced to say it is red, on the basis of its exact resemblance to S_{j-1}? The point of the argument just given is that observers are not constrained to say either of these things by any rules of sense to which they can reasonably be seen to be committed. They are free to go either way or even to refuse to say anything at all.

Thus tolerance rules cannot force us to paradoxical conclusions. Provided they are interpreted as loose rules containing an exception clause, they allow scope for individual judgement about difficult cases. Something which looks as much like its red neighbours as its orange ones differs in this respect from both, and this difference, being a relevant one, justifies the refusal to apply either predicate.

6.6 Strict and Loose Tolerance Rules

Only strict tolerance rules lead to paradox. But these cannot be true, even where the predicates are highly observational and there seems to be only one dimension to the appearance. Suppose someone judges that **a** is red and **b** matches it perfectly in colour. They are committed by the strict rule for "red" to saying that **b** is red also *whatever else may be the case*. But **b** may be indiscernible from **c** and they may judge **c** to be non-red. On strict tolerance rules they would be committed to contradictory conclusions as to the colour of **b**. But this only shows that strict tolerance rules are incoherent. For by those rules, **b**'s match with other things, apart from **a**, may be relevant to establishing its colour, just as relevant as its match with **a**. But, then, if the match with **a** is not the only thing which matters, it does not force the application of the predicate "red" *no matter what*. Multiple aspects of a thing's appearance with respect to colour must be allowed to count. So given the complexity of appearances, which can in particular cases be brought out by comparisons of this kind, various indiscernibilities may have to be weighed up. If indiscernibility is to matter at all in determining a thing's colour, it must do so according to loose rules.

So it is not appearances which are incoherent, but strict tolerance rules. Tolerance rules must therefore be of the kind suggested above. For "red" we will have:

> If one thing is red and a second is indistinguishable from it in colour then, provided there are no other relevant differences between the two, the second is red also.

Where the two are paradigmatically red there will not be any dissimilarity between them in terms of the indistinguishability of one but not the other from something marginally orange or pink or some other colour. But, where there is a difference of this kind, we are justified in doubting that both are red.

The claim that we are following loose rules which allow some scope for matters of judgement and stipulation fits the pattern of divergence and consistency in usage. For, confronted with a borderline case, it does seem equally correct to go either way: if one person says it is red and another says it isn't then there is no assumption that one is wrong or that they have not grasped the colour concepts involved. A casual observer might size things up either way since appearances are complex and different people may notice and weigh up the various relevant aspects of a thing's appearance differently. So it is possible coherently to explain and justify our managing to limit the scope of observational predicates. We can also explain in this way the degree of consistency which seems to exist in this area and which was so puzzling if our model were of a game whose participants broke the rules all the time. Now we need not suppose that we are in the grip of inconsistent rules: we have the model of a game played according to loose rules.

6.7 A Parallel with the Grue Paradox

The question of whether or not an observational predicate extends to one more member of a series must always involve inductive considerations. For, applying such a predicate to a newly encountered object or reapplying it after some object has changed involves inductive judgement: it must be determined that this case is sufficiently like ones to which the predicate was successfully applied in the past. When a change does and when it does not make a difference to the applicability of an observational predicate is not a matter to be determined by any strict, purely mechanical semantic rules. Loose guiding principles which remain sensitive to further evidence are the kind of rules which could plausibly be grasped and conveyed to others and, so, are the best candidates for substantial rules of the kind Wright is seeking for the use of these predicates.

It might be concluded from this that Wright's substantial rules have no place in a theory of meaning for a natural language. (This is the kind of conclusion Evans and McDowell would welcome.) Alternatively, it might be argued that there can be no very sharp distinction drawn between purely linguistic rules and inductive tests for the reapplicability of a predicate after change. Inductive coherence is part and parcel of overall linguistic coherence. (Putnam has explicitly argued for this claim in [1].) The connexion of meaning with understanding makes the second view the more attractive. We have been supposing all along that the meanings of expressions may be given by rules which determine their usage and, unless meaning is to be divorced from understanding, a grasp of those rules must be sufficient for mastery of the expressions they govern. It seems extremely plausible to suppose that rules sufficient for mastery of highly observational predicates would have an inductive component, for they are acquired as a result of inductive training in the recognition of appropriate similarities and differences.

These considerations lead to a view of the Sorites Paradox as not too unlike certain inductive puzzles. Both the Grue Paradox and the Sorites threaten trusted patterns of ordinary reasoning, though in the case of the first these have been taken to include commonly accepted inductive practices and in the case of the second, fundamental deductive principles. There is a structural similarity however, since both paradoxes have to do with the scope and limits of observational predicates and both raise, in an acute form, the question of when a predicate which has been correctly applied to a series of similar things may safely be projected to the next in the series. In both cases the answer that we are following certain simple rules results in paradox and contradiction. An object is grue if and only if it is either examined before a specified date and found to be green or else not examined before that date and blue. So all examined emeralds are grue. Contradiction results where "gruelike" predicates are projected beyond the evidence class according to the straight rule and where strict tolerance rules are used to project ordinary predicates from one member of a Sorites series to the next. And it seems that in both cases there is a plausible solution to the paradox if the overly simple rule is replaced by one which is more sensitive to actual linguistic and inductive practices. (See Goodman [1], pp.72f, for an account of this paradox.)

So the Grue Paradox and the Sorites are similar in that both raise questions about formulating rules which permit the projection of an observational predicate from examined members of a series to further members, and the paradoxes arise in both cases from answers which fail to reflect the complexity of the inductive situation. The problem with the grue predicate concerns the straight rule (SR): the practice of arguing from certain objects (the evidence class) possessing some property to the conclusion that some other objects (the consequent class) have the property also. But we must have a grasp of what previous cases had in common which led us to apply the predicate to them and be on the look-out for disanalogies with the new case. Where the new one lacks what the others had in common it ought not to be characterized in the same way. It may be argued then that the straight rule needs amending.

In an article in the Journal of Philosophy, 1975, Frank Jackson suggests the straight rule should read as follows:[56] *certain Fs being G supports, by the SR, other Fs being G, but certain Fs which are H being G does not support other Fs which are not H being G; in each case the reason being that it is known that the Fs that form the evidence class would not have been G if they had not been H.*

This formula solves the Grue Paradox for, if the emeralds in the evidence class had not been examined before the year 2,000 (or whatever date is specified in the definition of grueness), they would not have been grue. On the other hand, the emeralds in the evidence class would still have been green if they had not been examined by that date. Examining things does not alter their colour. Green may therefore be projected to unexamined emeralds, but grue may not.

The apparent inevitability of the Sorites Paradox depends upon accepting the overly simple strict version of the tolerance rules. Loose tolerance rules provide a way out of the dilemma, and the

---

[56] Jackson [2], p.123.

general schema for these rules is structurally similar to Jackson's reformulation of the straight rule. For we said that where two things were indistinguishable with respect to a group of determining concepts for a predicate which applied to one, it would apply to the other also *unless* they differed in some further relevant respect. Relevance could, we argued, be captured in terms of a conditional (see section 6.4), and it turns out to be very similar to the one italicised just above. In actual series exhibiting smooth continuity in some dimensions of appearance the predicate H will be a relational one: where ϕ is a determining concept for the predicate F, H will be "indiscernibility with respect to ϕ"; a predicate which holds between some pairs of members of the series but not others.

Chapter 7

FURTHER PROBLEMS AND PUZZLES

7.1 Is Indiscernibility Tolerant?

Those who have been impressed by the problem as it is presented by Dummett and Wright may remain unconvinced by the arguments against the incoherence thesis developed in the last chapter. They may object that indiscernibility itself (and its negation) may be tolerant and so exactly the same problems will arise at the higher level with respect to this relation. And so they will challenge the argument at the point where it is claimed that since some members of the series have the property of being just discernibly different from the initial member, there will be a sharp break somewhere in a determining respect for the predicate being projected. For, if indiscernibility is tolerant this property of being indiscernible from S_1 will apply to any member of a suitably finely gradated series provided it applies to the one before. Then there will not be a first to have the property of barely discernible difference from S_1 for if one member is indiscernible from S_1, the next will be also.

The claim that there cannot be a sharp break anywhere between members in terms of their indiscernibility from end members of the series need not carry a commitment to the view that indiscernibility behaves transitively throughout. If the end members of a series are to be discernibly different from each other with respect to ϕ, then indiscernibility in that respect cannot behave transitively at every point throughout the series. But it seems possible to imagine series in which definite cases of non-transitive indiscernibility are to be found only between widely-spaced members with no instances anywhere of immediate neighbours differing in their indiscernibility from any third thing. So the existence of apparently continuous series whose end members differ in some observable respect means only that the following general transitivity principle must be rejected:

$$\text{G.T.}\quad (\forall x)(\forall y)(\forall o)((\text{Ind}\phi(x,y,o) \rightarrow (\forall z)(\text{Ind}\phi(y,z,o)) \rightarrow \text{Ind}\phi(x,z,o))$$

(where x and y range over any objects and o over observers and "$Ind_{\phi}(x,y,o)$" is to be read as "x is indiscernible from y with respect to ϕ to observer o"). But if indiscernibility is tolerant there should be some set of series which are so finely gradated with respect to ϕ that the following principle holds for any series S_{ϕ} in the set:

A.T. $(\forall x)(\forall y)(\forall z)(\forall o)(x,y,z \in S_{\phi} \ \& \ AdjS_{\phi}(x,y) \rightarrow (Ind_{\phi}(y,z,o) \rightarrow Ind_{\phi}(x,z,o)))$

(where "$AdjS_{\phi}(x,y)$" means "x and y are adjacent members of the series S_{ϕ}")[57]

One reason which might be offered for thinking that there must be some set of series for which A.T. holds is that "indiscernible for o with respect to ϕ" and "just discernibly different to o with respect to ϕ" seem to be highly observational predicates and so we might expect them to be tolerant. However this case differs in several ways from the other observational predicates discussed by Wright. It does seem plausible (at least initially) to suppose that if the predicate "red" applies to one member of a colour series which alters sufficiently gradually, then the next member deserves it also. For adjacent members will look the same to ordinary observers, and a colour predicate should apply to both of a pair of things indiscernible in appearance in all relevant respects. But to claim indiscernibility is tolerant is to claim that if the pair <x,y> are indiscernible to an observer, and y and z are neighbours in an apparently continuous series, then the pair <y,z> must be indiscernible to that observer also. And it is not plausible to suppose that if the one pair is indiscernible to some observer they will invariably find the other indiscernible also since it is a matter of plain empirical fact that observers sometimes do notice differences between the first and the third members of triads of this kind.

Secondly, it is difficult even to make sense of the notion of tolerance for these relational predicates[58] To claim that indiscernibility is a tolerant predicate would have to be to claim that there could be a series whose members are *pairs* of objects

---

57 Exactly which series these are is a matter to be determined by an empirical study of just noticeable differences.

58 Dummett makes this point in [2]

meeting certain conditions. The first member of such a series would have to be a pair of things which are indiscernible in some respect, and the last member would have to consist of a pair of things which are discernibly different in the same respect. Furthermore there would have to be a relation between one pair and the next such that if any pair is accepted as indiscernible, the next must be admitted to be indiscernible also. The problem is to find a plausible notion of indiscernibility holding *between* consecutive pairs which we could use to argue that if one pair is (internally) indiscernible and this relation of (external) indiscernibility (whatever it is) holds between the pairs, then the second must be (internally) indiscernible also. And there seems to be no sense in which two *pairs* of things could be called indiscernible from one another with respect to some property ϕ. Perhaps the best way of making sense of a claim that two pairs were indiscernible would be to assume that each of the four things composing the pairs was indiscernible from each of the others. This is not the sense we want, since it involves assuming what is to be proven: to argue that the predicate is tolerant we have to make use of the relation of indiscernibility-between-pairs and the internal indiscernibility of the first pair to show that the second pair is indiscernible also. If indiscernibility between pairs has to be construed as indiscernibility between all members of both pairs, the second pair will of course consist of indiscernible items. It seems impossible to find any other non-question begging construal of the notion of indiscernibility between pairs.

However, there may be other ways of construing the objection and of arguing for A.T. which do not involve claiming that indiscernibility is tolerant in exactly the way other non-relational predicates are tolerant. What would be required to counter any such replies, based on possible interpretations of tolerance, is a proof that A.T. is false, that is, that there is no set of series so finely gradated that if any member x is indiscernible from an end member of the series for some observer, so is the successor of x. To show that there is no such set of series would be to show that indiscernibility could not be tolerant (on any reasonable construal of what that claim meant).

The argument against A.T. is identical with the proof of (i) - (iii) given in 6.5, for A.T. consists simply in denying the conjunction of these three propositions. The argument for (i) - (iii) is that an observer who sees that the end members of a series look different from one another in some respect and who judges certain intervening members to be indiscriminable in that respect from an end member has to start finding a difference from that end member somewhere. For if every succeeding member looked indiscriminable from the first one could find no difference between the end members. Somewhere along the series an observer must notice a difference from an end member. So A.T. must be false and (i) - (iii) true.

The claim made in 6.5 that the indiscernibility predicate must be sharply bounded is still in need of further argument however. For although the argument that it is tolerant fails, the more moderate claim that indiscernibility is at least vague in *some* sense fitting our original definition may seem plausible. According to that definition a predicate is vague if its applicability can be made to fade away gradually. If indiscernibility was shown to be vague in some sense fitting this definition Sorites arguments might be revived. To investigate this possibility we must examine the relation between vagueness and tolerance and consider whether "indiscernible from" is a vague predicate.

7.2 Is Indiscernibility Vague?

Can indiscernibility from an end member of a series be made to fade away gradually without there being any particular member of the series which is definitely the last to have it? If it can, then in a sufficiently finely gradated series there is no natural point at which we can say; "Here the strips begin to look just noticeably different with respect to ϕ from S_1". There will, it seems, be no sharp break in terms of any determining concept between one member of the series and the next.

It seems plausible to suppose indiscernibility is vague in this Fregean sense because of examples of the following kind. Suppose that two things which at first appeared to *all* observers to be indiscernible in some easily observable aspect could alter so gradually that although they looked discernibly different to those observers in the end, it would not be possible to say *in general* where they begin to differ. Examples can easily be imagined of subtle variation in the shape or shade of two images on a screen. That is, different observers asked to say when the image began to differ in appearance would select different points. This is made plausible by the fact that powers of discrimination vary from observer to observer. If indiscernibility can be made to fade away gradually in this fashion it is vague in our original sense of lacking sharp boundaries. It would not be plausible to pick out one particular frame as the last in which the two appeared indiscernible, for different observers would select other frames as the last.

Also, each individual observer shown the same series several times over might select different frames each time if asked to pick out the last in which the two images appeared indiscernible. The discriminatory abilities of a single individual fluctuate from time to time depending on concentration, fatigue, attention, motivation etc.

So we may grant the vagueness of indiscernibility in this sense: there is no laying down sharp limits to its scope in any context since the limit of possible discriminations will vary over a certain range. It may follow from this that the class of counter-examples to G.T. is ill-defined. We would surely not want to say, however, that an observer who judged a pair of images of the above kind to be indiscernible in the relevant respect at one moment would be bound to judge them indiscernible at the next also. For if they look different to that person at the next moment what is to force them to say otherwise? There is (obviously) a relevant respect in which the two differ. So the predicates "indiscernible (to anyone) with respect to ϕ" and "indiscernible to observer O with respect to ϕ" may be vague according to one (weak) interpretation of Frege's definition, but they are not tolerant. Vagueness of this sort clearly cannot produce incoherence and Sorites problems of the sort we are investigating. This difference between vagueness and tolerance is obscured by an unclarity in Wright's and Dummett's arguments concerning *who* is not permitted by rules of sense for vague predicates to draw sharp limits to their application. It is unclear whether their arguments are meant to establish that the theorist can determine no definite unique limits to the extension of vague predicates, or whether the ordinary users of the language are constrained by rules they have accepted to refuse to call a halt at any point to the application of a vague predicate. If their argument establishes only the first, then the absence of sharp boundaries to the correct scope of vague predicates leaves ordinary language users free in particular contexts to draw limits at various points within the hazy range. We shall consider both interpretations in chapter 9.

The question is whether there is a stronger sense in which the predicates lack sharp boundaries. Could there be a series which varied so gradually that if an ordinary observer ever felt justified in judging at any point that a member differed discernibly from the initial member they would feel bound to say that the one immediately before it was discriminably different from that first member also? We know that observers will at some point notice for the first time that some member of the series is discernibly different from the first. They may then feel bound to retract the judgement that the one before this was indiscernible from the first. They may also wish to retract the judgement that the one before that was indiscernible from the first and so on. But we know that this process is bound to come to an end: as they work back they will find one which does look indiscernible from the first.

Observers may, of course, come across some items which leave them uncertain about what to say. It may not seem right to say that they are indiscernible from the first or to say that they are just discernibly different from it. And presumably, where they find a sharp break between any two members in a series in terms of their indiscernibility from an end member it will always be possible to insert suitable intervening members so as to create uncertainty of this kind. Does this possibility revive the Paradox?

This is a by now familiar move: in setting up the problem at the beginning it was argued that wherever a difference relevant to the application of an observational predicate is discernible between members of a series the difference could be diminished by inserting more members. Human powers of discrimination being limited, the difference is bound to disappear sooner or later. The argument seemed plausible at the lower level but as we shall soon see, differences from member to member in terms of their indiscernibility from others cannot be made to fade away in the same fashion as lower order differences.

Suppose S_i and S_{i-1} are adjacent members of a series and are indiscernible with respect to ϕ but differ in that S_{i-1} is also indiscernible in the same respect from S_1 and S_i is not. Let $S_{i-0.5}$ be a suitable intermediate item, indiscernible from both S_i and S_{i-1}, and suppose it is inserted between them. There are just three things, it seems, which an observer could say about its relation to S_1. They may say $S_{i-0.5}$ is indiscernible from S_1, they may say it is just discernibly different from S_1, or they may say that it does not seem right to say either of these things. In the first case $S_{i-0.5}$ will differ significantly from S_i. If it is just discernibly different from S_1, it will differ in a significant respect from S_{i-1}. And in the third case it will differ significantly from both its immediate neighbours. For S_{i-1} does look indiscernible from S_1, and S_{i-1} does not. We have shown above that indiscernibility with respect to ϕ is a determining concept for any predicate for which ϕ is a determining concept and so wherever a determining concept for a predicate extends to one thing and it is an indeterminate matter whether or not it extends to a second thing, there is a difference between the two in a respect relevant to the application of that predicate. When all other determining factors are equal this difference may leave an observer unsure whether or not to apply the predicate to the second thing. So it is at least reasonable to say that it is a borderline case. Whether or not the observable difference is a large enough one to warrant the determinate refusal to apply the predicate is a matter to be weighed up by individual observers.

Further intermediate items could always be inserted where there is a difference of one of these three kinds between $S_{i-0.5}$ and its neighbours. But then the same questions would arise. It might be claimed however, that the range of available answers widens with each expansion of the series. It may turn out that between things indiscernible from S_1 and and ones only indeterminately indiscernible from it there are things which can be described as indeterminately indeterminate in respect of indiscernibility from S_1: these would exist in a fringe area between the things clearly indiscernible from S_1 and the things only indeterminately indiscernible from it. Perhaps there are further, even finer, distinctions to be drawn. There must be limits to these fine distinctions though, for there are surely limits to the fineness of the discriminations which human observers are capable of making. But now this point, which was used to support the view we are arguing against, can be used here to prove that there have to be limits to the vagueness of indiscernibility and just discernible difference, points at which it becomes evident that there is a difference which was not evident before.

Suppose there is no distinguishing things indeterminately indeterminately indiscernible from S_1 from things which are just indeterminately indiscernible from it. Then there is no real distinction here: both kinds of things are just indeterminately indiscernible from S_1. Any further items inserted between them will be also. This means that anything inserted between an object indiscernible from S_1 and one which is only indeterminately indiscernible from it will have to fall on one side or the other of this division: there are no further finer distinctions to be made. So each attempt to smooth over a sharp break between adjacent members of a series will either produce further relevant division or else leave the original break unchanged.

Also, the observer's uncertainty about whether or not to call members indiscernible from the first in some stretches of the series is bound to be resolved at some point. They will have to say of some members that they do and of others that they do not have this relation to the first. And so there will be a difference at that point between one member to the next with respect to a determining concept for the non-relational predicate being projected through the series.

7.3 Inconsistency without Paradox

The paradox may be resolved, we have argued, and the incoherence thesis shown to be false if it is possible to justify the actions of an observer of a finely gradated series who draws sharp limits somewhere in the series to the application of an observational predicate which clearly applies to some members. We have argued that their delimiting the boundaries of the predicate is consistent with its being a tolerant predicate for tolerance principles must be seen to be loose rather than strict rules. So long as there is a difference somewhere from one member to the next in a respect relevant to the application of the predicate the observer is justified in refusing to apply the predicate beyond that point. We argued that an observer would, at some point, spot a difference of this sort between two adjacent members: since indiscernibility behaves non-transitively one but not the other will be indiscernible from some third member of the series.

What is an observer to say about an object which has an exact resemblance to things which when compared closely appear to be of different shades of colour? We argued in the last chapter that an observer would be justified in calling the object a borderline case. They may say of it that it is indeterminate in colour between red and orange, for example, and refuse to apply either label to it. Or they may say it is either one. The policy they adopt will depend upon the context: if the exact description of its colour matters in the context they will probably go for the former description: if it is unimportant they will say either that it is red or that it is orange.

It is more likely, of course, that there will be a number of strips towards the middle which seem equally deserving of either colour predicate. In a very finely gradated series this will always be the case. But no matter how gradual the variation in shade we will eventually arrive at a strip which is indiscriminable in colour from one which looks to us like a borderline case. Since the rules which determine the application of observational predicates are loose ones, we not forced to say that it is a borderline case also for we had decided that the strip before it was red. This one strikes us differently from the ones on either side. We may say it is red or say that it is a borderline case also.

There is a third variety of possible descriptions of the objects towards the middle of the series and it is one which appears to raise some problems for our argument. So far the claim has been that if we see ourselves as following vague but coherent rules we can avoid contradictions and paradox. But there would seem to be nothing about the loose tolerance rules which would prevent an observer from describing the unclear cases towards the middle of the series as deserving of *both* predicates. It seems inconsistent however to describe these strips as both red and orange, since colour predicates are presumed to exclude one another. But these strips between the clear cases of the application of "red" and the clear cases of the application of "orange" resemble the things on either side: our argument would seem to justify the observer who applied both predicates to the same object in one context.

The best reply here is simply to concede the point. Surely no-one should expect natural language to be perfectly coherent. Any incoherence has the consequence that applications of the language which may be justified on reasonable grounds can sometimes lead to contradictory conclusions. It seems plausible to accept on the basis of the meanings of colour terms both the exclusivity of those terms and their joint application in certain cases. Our only task was to refute the claim that natural language is radically incoherent, that widespread contradictions result from our inability to contain the application of observational terms within any limits. A moderate amount of inconsistency is to be expected in any language containing observational terms and does not establish that natural languages are radically inconsistent and generate irresoluble paradoxes of the kind discussed above.

7.4 Patches in Pairs

It would be possible to present the observer of the colour series with strips in discrete pairs so that no observable differences in terms of indiscernibilities from other things are evident. Suppose the pairs are shown in random order or with such large breaks in between that there is no possibility of the observer accurately comparing the colours of the strips in memory. We could imagine that indiscriminably coloured pairs are flashed onto a screen one pair at a time, in such a way that the left-hand member of each pair is identical with the right-hand member of some other pair. (That is, the pairs have overlapping members.) At some point an observer will refuse to apply a colour predicate to some pair, perhaps despite having applied it to both of a previously seen pair having a member in common with this one.

This presents no difficulties for our argument. The inconsistency over the common member of the two pairs may be argued to be an inevitable consequence of the looseness of fit of observational predicates to the world. Someone who applies a colour predicate to an object in one context may refuse to apply it to the same unchanged object in another context. The observer can only be forced by Sorites arguments to conclude that inconsistent predicates apply *throughout* the series if further members are introduced in the same visual context so that the indiscernibility of other members of overlapping pairs is evident. But in that case they could also find *differences* from member to member which would permit them to avoid those wide ranging contradictions. The appearance of visually isolated pairs may vary from context to context: it is only where the visual context is one of smoothly continuous change that it can be argued with any plausibility that an observer may be led by Sorites arguments into contradictions.

7.5 The Size of the Difference

There may be a further worry here that although the observable differences from member to member in terms of indiscernibilities from further members of the series are of a kind which is *relevant* to questions about the colour of each, they will often be *too small* to matter in deciding those questions. To warrant a break in the applicability of a predicate there would have to be a sizeable difference in some relevant respect: here, the difference is barely discernible. Where the difference between one thing and the next as they are directly compared is admitted to be discernible, the problem is to say how large the relational difference between them with respect to other objects must be to be sufficient to justify the application of the predicate to one but not the other.

There is something odd about this problem, since it coincides with the following question: how great must be the similarity between two things if we are to classify them as falling under the same observational predicate? There is no answer to this except the uninteresting one that resemblances and differences between things are large enough to matter in this way when they are large enough to be noticed and taken to matter to the applicability of the predicate by most observers. (How red do things have to be to be red? How closely must they resemble the shades of postboxes or red roses? The answer can only be: red enough for most people to count them as red. Or alternatively; distinguishably redder in colour than everything taken to be orange or pink or some other colour.)

The best explanation of an observer's refusal to apply a colour predicate past some point in a series is surely that after this things start to resemble too closely clear instances of a different colour predicate. Since previously examined members of the series had not been judged to have this degree of resemblance to things falling under the other predicate the difference must be large enough to matter. In many cases small observable differences do not matter; why they do matter when they do has no philosophically interesting general explanation other than that they add up to a difference large enough to oblige a different classification.

7.6 A Review of the Criteria of Justification

What will actually happen when an observer does detect a difference of this sort? It may perhaps seem unrealistic to suppose that they will find a triad meeting these conditions, that is, whose third member is imbedded somewhere in or at the end of the series and is seen to be indiscernible from one but not the other of the first two adjacent members. Indiscernibility and just noticeable differences are difficult to detect for one thing: we cannot assume that a casual observer will be attending sufficiently to notice these fine differences between adjacent members. Also, if the series is very finely gradated it might be extremely long and the third member of the triad too distant for it to be physically possible to compare it with the other two adjacent members.

These problems are not too serious however. Indiscernibility is a limiting case of resemblance, and an object's resemblance, or lack of resemblance, to other things which clearly deserve a certain predicate is surely relevant to determining whether or not the predicate extends to it also. Where a number of objects have been classified as red and then we come across one which seems to resemble non-red things as much as red ones, this difference from the previously classified ones is sufficient to warrant a break in the applicability of the predicate. If this is accepted it can now be seen that recognition of an exact match between this new object and some particular later member of the series is not important. It is enough if this one strikes the observer as resembling non-red objects too closely to be clearly red and none of the previously examined members of the series had looked that way. Normal adult observers with a grasp of the use of predicates like "red" do not need to be presented with further objects for comparison in order to judge that something resembles clear cases of the application of a predicate.

We can therefore relax the requirement that in order to justify calling a halt to the scope of an observational predicate in a series an observer must recognize a difference between members on either side in terms of their indiscernibility from some third member of that series. If the argument of the last chapter is correct there will be a difference of this sort which observers are capable of recognizing, but we need not insist they go to this much trouble in order to be justified in their refusal to apply a predicate passed a certain point. To actually recognize a difference in these terms between adjacent members would, of course, be sufficient to warrant the non-application of the relevant predicate to one of the pair but certain weaker conditions are sufficient also. In general we may say that whenever an observer has applied an observational predicate to some members of a series and then notices that further members look different from the previously examined ones in some respect relevant to the application of that predicate, they are justified in refusing to apply it any longer.

7.7 Conceptual and Metaphysical Miracles

In sections 4.3 and 5.4 we outlined Unger's version of the Sorites argument. We shall look briefly now at the consequences of the above arguments for his claims concerning the following triad of propositions:

(1) There is at least one stone.

(2) For anything there may be, if it is a stone, then it consists of some large but finite number of atoms.

(3) For anything there may be, if it is stone, then the net removal of one atom, or only a few, in a way which is most innocuous and favourable will not mean the difference as to whether or not there is a stone in the situation.

Unger claims that these propositions are inconsistent and since (2) and (3) are undeniably true, (1) must be rejected. (3) must be taken as asserting or in some way implying that there are in the case of stones innocuous means of atomic removal, that is, means which leave a stone's identity unaffected; in the light of the arguments of the last chapter this premiss may seem dubious. Unger claims that the denial of this premiss does not make sense: there are always ways (probably millions of them) of removing at least one atom without going from there being a stone to there being no stone. To think otherwise, he says, is to believe in miracles. One such miracle, the miracle of metaphysical illusion, would involve the preservation of ordinary things by sudden breaks in nature. It might prove to be impossible to remove any more atoms after the first million, say, have been ticked off. Or the stone might suddenly change into a frog. The other miracle he ridicules involves believing that the concepts we employ have extraordinarily precise limits. This he calls "the miracle of conceptual comprehension". Both these miracles must be rejected, he says, the first because of our knowledge of gradual change in the world and the second because we know that ordinary thought is imprecise. "Concept", for Unger as for Wright, is used in a pre-philosophical ordinary sense, in which it cannot be denied that many of our concepts are vague. No-one could seriously believe that our concept of a stone (in this sense of "concept") discriminates between stones and non-stones at an atomic level.

The question of the truth of the premiss that for an object of any ordinary kind there is always some identity-preserving deletion of its matter involves various issues to do with the determination of reference of natural kind terms which are not touched upon at all by Unger. If we consider the question of whether as a matter of empirical fact there is always, for each individual observer and any given object accepted by that observer as a thing of a particular sort, some deletion of matter from the object which would leave that observer's counting the object as still a thing of that sort, then the answer is clearly negative. After some deletion at some time the observer will no longer accept the thing as a thing of that sort. This will hold no matter how small we make the deletion. Precisely where an observer calls a halt to the application of a natural kind predicate will depend, however, on a vast number of unknown determinants including individual perceptual factors, context and the individual's past history of application of the predicate. The moment at which the combined effect of these determines the individual's rejection of the predicate will coincide with some stage in the process of atomic removal, but there will obviously be a huge range of variation here from observer to observer, and in the decisions made by a single observer in different contexts. Individual atomic removals are too fine-grained to count as causal factors in the altering of the individual's perception of the object as a thing of a certain kind, though the alteration of their perception of the object is a consequence of the combined effect of a vast number of them together with other factors. It is true, then, that single atomic deletions all on their own, other relevant factors remaining fixed, are identity-preserving. But, since these tiny deletions of matter inevitably coincide with other alterations which do have a direct causal influence on the individual's perception of the object it is not true that after each stage an individual's verdict on the status of the object will be unchanged.

So if we conceive of "innocuous and favourable" ways of removing atoms as ones which are accompanied by no other changes causally relevant to the observer's perception of the object as a thing of that sort, Unger's third premiss is true. But its antecedent, understood as implying all other relevant factors are to remain fixed, will not be fulfilled. Atomic removals which are in themselves innocuous will inevitably coincide at some stage with identity-threatening alterations. It does seem necessary to interpret the third premiss in this way, as containing a ceteris paribus clause, for it to be at all plausible, for otherwise we could imagine situations in which, for example, the stone is utterly pulverised at the instant the peripheral atom is gently removed. Where this occurs all will agree that there is a stone no longer. The same intepretation of "innocuous and favourable" obviously holds for any application of Unger's argument to ordinary things. If a wombat insists on crossing the Hume highway at the time a single atom is removed and is squashed flat at that instant we will say there is no longer a wombat in the situation. So on this interpretation (3) is true but not inconsistent with (1) and (2). To get an inconsistent set we need the further premiss that no other changes take place which are relevant to the identity of the object and this premiss is not true.

Thus atomic removals will not on their own make a difference as to whether or not there is a stone present, but they will at some time inevitably coincide with alterations which do affect the individual's perception of an object as a thing of a certain sort. Suddenly, after some vast number of atomic removals, the thing will no longer look sufficently stonelike to warrant the application of the predicate.

Of course the question of the continued existence of the stone is not determined by the decision of any individual observer to withhold the application of the predicate. But the individual decisions must be seen as shifting the communal response to the depleted object and the weight of communal opinion must settle the question eventually. In the case of natural kind predicates differences in superficial appearance available to ordinary members of a community matter less in deciding questions about applicability than in the instances of highly observational qualitative predicates considered in the last chapter. What does decide the question varies greatly from one natural kind term to another. Whether or not two things both count as gold depends not on appearance and community decision but on atomic structure. The characteristics which count for the application of the natural kind terms of biology and zoology or for terms like "person" are likely to involve both precise genetic features as well as appearance and typical behaviour. Not every mass of platypus genetic material is a platypus, nor is everything which appears to be a platypus a genuine member of that species. Internal structure and style of reproduction matter also. But since there is no theory of the platypus which could deliver a clear-cut answer to the question of when in the series of atomic removals a platypus ceases to exist, the decision will have to rest in the end upon the rough concensus of trained observers.

It seems not to be true then, that for each observer there is always some removal of matter so innocuous as to leave their judgement of the status of the object unaltered for although innocuous on their own, atomic removals are inevitably accompanied at some point by identity-threatening changes in appearance. And the negative answer to this question does bear on the answer to the question Unger raises (abstracting from individual observers) concerning the preservation of identity of things through insubstantial change. Whether or not there is still a thing of a particular kind after such a change depends at least in part on appearances and so on the judgements of observers, on which numerous complex contextual factors will bear. A wombat only continues to exist at some time and place if there is something then and there which answers to our communal conception of a wombat.[59]

The variable effects of these determining features go to show that no miracles have been performed. Observers will draw limits to the continued existence of the animal at different stages in the series of minute removals envisaged by Unger. The weight of communal opinion in one context need not carry any implications for future applications of the predicate, either on the part of individuals or the same community as a whole, in other contexts. So there is no justification for saying that just because everyone will agree, eventually, in any particular context to call a halt somewhere to the application of a term that their shared conception discriminates absurdly finely. Obviously it does not discriminate at the atomic level between wombats and non-wombats, and the roughness of such conceptions means that there will be a supply of alternative equally good answers to the question of whether or not there is still a wombat at some particular stage.

So this kind of answer does not involve supposing that there are sharp breaks in nature. One atom here or there makes no difference in general to the question of whether or not there is a stone (or a wombat) before us but it is nevertheless legitimate to draw limits at some point. A large range of alternative limits may be drawn, for the looseness of fit of such conceptions does *not* mean, as Unger assumes it does, that no answers are acceptable if they involve drawing sharp limits. Differences in terms of resemblances to clear and unclear cases of the application of the term can be recognized by observers and are surely relevant in determining a wide range of reasonable responses to such questions.

7.8 Vagueness and Pure Observationality

The arguments of the last chapter designed to resolve the Sorites Paradox leave us with several puzzles concerning perception and the existence of purely observational predicates. The reductio argument of 6.1 against pure observationality seems unsatisfactory now in the light of the adoption of loose rather than strict tolerance rules. For the original reductio argument, against Wright's assumption that such purely observational

---

[59] Unger's argument is of course designed to show that this concept is incoherent, but can only establish this if the deletion issue raised by premiss (3) can be resolved in his favour.

predicates exist was that if they did they would have to be tolerant and no tolerant predicate can be purely observational. The latter half of the argument depends on Sorites reasoning to establish that tolerant predicates can be forced to apply where competent observers would judge that they did not apply. If the judgements of competent observers concerning the application of a predicate may be overridden in this way, the predicate cannot be purely observational. We argued therefore, in the first section of chapter 6, that there can be no purely observational predicates.

However the arguments in the later sections of the last chapter - that observational predicates are governed by loose rather than strict tolerance rules - undermine the grounds for this conclusion. For suppose there exist some purely observational predicates (predicates standardly applied just on the basis of observation) and they are governed just by loose tolerance rules. It is not possible to argue now on the basis of those rules that they must apply beyond the limits which observers are willing to accept. And so there are no grounds for denying the existence of purely observational predicates.

It is not clear, however, that the arguments of the last chapter designed to establish the coherence of observational predicates in general can be applied to predicates which are purely observational in Wright's sense. If this is so, it seems possible to reinstate Wright's and Dummett's arguments for the incoherence of any language which has a purely observational part. We shall discuss this further problem in the next chapter.

Chapter 8

VAGUENESS AND PERCEPTION

8.1 A Puzzle about Perception

It was argued in chapter 6 that there is no need to see observational language as incoherent if the rules by which its predicates are governed are taken to be loose tolerance rules containing *ceteris paribus* clauses. For rules of this sort do not always force us to apply an observational predicate, such as "heap", to an object discernible by direct comparison with something we have admitted to be a heap. We are only bound to apply the predicate to both if it is applied to one and the pair are indiscernible in all respects relevant to the application of the predicate. Loose rules allow indiscernibility from some third thing (which we might not want to call a heap) to count also as a relevant respect to be weighed up. The original pair may be judged to differ significantly in this respect. The application of the predicate depends upon the judgement of individual observers who are competent in the sense that they coincide, on the whole, in their judgements with other normal observers who share the same language. So no strict mechanically applicable rules determine the use of observational predicates in all circumstances.

We argued above that if this is so, it is possible to accept a plausible version of the tolerance rules yet avoid the paradox. An observer confronted with a Sorites series may decide that some pair of adjacent members are indistinguishable in size and shape and that one is a heap and yet deny, quite consistently, that the other is a heap also. For the other may be indistinguishable in size and other relevant respects from some third thing which the observer is not happy to call a heap.

Although this move seems to make sense of observational language and provide an account of ourselves as operating with consistent principles in our application of observational predicates, it may be felt that some incoherence remains. It is not clear whether this solution applies to purely observational predicates (in Wright's sense or to predicates which are satisfied by phenomenal properties.[60] If a appears to an observer to be some shade of colour and b appears indistinguishable from it in shade, then surely b appears to be that same shade also, whatever else may be the case about their indiscernibility in shade from other things. Supposing phenomenal shade predicates to be available, it seems that any such predicate must apply to both a and b if it applies to either. So then the question arises: what justification could there be for refusing to apply such predicates past some point on a Sorites colour series if things indiscernible to the observer were to be found on either side of it?

This problem emerges in the form of well-known puzzle in the philosophy of perception. It is possible to find triads of things which appear so alike in colour to some observer that they judge the first to be indiscernible in colour from the second and the second to be indiscernible from the third, although they are just able to discern a difference in shade between the first and the third. The following three statements would then seem to be true at the same time:

(i) a and b appear to observer O to be uniformly the same shade of colour

(ii) b and c appear to observer O to be uniformly the same shade of colour

(iii) a and c appear to O to be uniformly different shades of colour

(We take "uniformly" here to mean that the item exhibits no variation in shade of colour.) Call the shade that a appears to be S_a and the shade that c appears to be S_c: how are we to avoid paradoxical conclusions such as

(iv) b appears to O to be two distinct shades of colour all over ?

We could also conclude that b is both S_a and not S_a, since it is indiscernible from something which is that shade and from something which is not that shade.

Arguments about tolerance rules seem irrelevant here, since the paradoxical argument concerns the appearances of things rather than applications of language. In the case of the Sorites the incoherence could be blamed on language and, as we admitted

[60]The differences between these are discussed in section 8.2

earlier, it seems just possible that langauge users might have accepted a set of inconsistent rules. But the way the world appears to be is surely an aspect of the world rather than language. There cannot be incoherence, then, in the way things appear to us to be. But if no inconsistent state of affairs could appear to obtain, how are we to explain away the above perceptual paradox?

There are six possible solutions to this paradox which seem worth discussing. These positions, and some of the more obvious difficulties with each are outlined below.

1) The argument is often taken as showing that there are no sense data or at least no phenomenal properties. For if we take appearances - sensa - seriously, as things that exist in the world, we seem driven to the conclusion that they have contradictory properties.

So although we cannot rely on the *reductio* argument of 6.1 as grounds for rejecting pure observationality, we might use the existence of this version of the paradox as establishing that at any rate purely observational predicates cannot be satisfied by phenomenal properties. We could then agree with Dummett's view of the Sorites paradox as showing that there cannot be any phenomenal properties while disagreeing with some of his arguments for this which are designed to show that observational language is incoherent.

This may be thought unsatisfactory for a number of reasons. It may be argued that the analysis of perceptual experience requires the existence of private sensory items of some kind. Non-veridical perceptions - sensory illusions, after-images, dreams and hallucinations - do not seem easily explicable on any other account of perception. Also, it seems impossible to deny that perception has a sensory element: to refuse to admit the existence of sense data might seem to amount to denying this. The final, and most serious, objection to this popular response is that it does not seem to remove the difficulty. Even if there are no entities with the properties sense data have been supposed to have there is still a problem about making sense of observers' reports of their visual experiences: (i), (ii) and (iii) seem to be truths whatever one says at a more theoretical level about perception.

2) It appears possible at first sight to avoid the problem by arguing that our sense data may have some properties of

which we are not perceptually aware. Suppose a_1, b_1 and c_1 are sensory items corresponding in some appropriate way to the objects a, b and c respectively. It could be argued that b_1 is a third phenomenal shade, distinct from that of either a_1 or c_1.

We shall argue below (in section 8.2) that this is not a satisfactory way out for the sense datum theorist. Not only does it undermine the point of having a sense datum theory, it leads (as we shall see) to the conclusion that we are never aware of phenomenal shades. The existence of appearances of things (of which we are aware) must be denied, and so this line collapses into (1).

3) Some sense datum theorists have argued for the following solution. The argument goes wrong, they claim, in supposing that the sensory item corresponding to b in (i) above (the sensory item we have when we look at b and a together) is the same sensory item as that which correponds to b in (ii),(the item which results when we perceive b and c). It is wrong to assume that the sensory item corresponding to b when it is seen together with a is identical in colour to the other sensory item corresponding to b when it is seen together with c. In fact this cannot be so: it is logically impossible for the two sensory items corresponding to b to be the same shade of colour, for they are identical in colour with things which are different shades.

This intriguing solution might be used to resolve the Sorites argument in the more general form discussed in earlier chapters. It depends, however, on a large assumption *viz* that at least one member of the series alters in appearance as we compare it with its neighbours on either side. This assumption appears to be a straightforwardly empirical one which may or may not be correct, and so the claim that it is logically impossible for things to be otherwise seems dubious. There may be other ways out of the problem. We shall argue in 8.3 that some other way must be found since this solution will not work.

4) We might try rejecting the argument on other grounds. One moral of the previous chapters should be that appearances are complex and have a structure, even in the most

> apparently simple "one-dimensional" cases. Bearing this in mind we might argue that the predicate "is the same phenomenal shade as a_1" applies to b_1 only if there are no differences to be observed between a_1 and b_1 which are relevant to questions about their phenomenal shades. Since there is such a relevant observable difference between a_1 and b_1 in the visual context described above, (one but not the other being indiscernable in shade from c_1), an observer would be justified in withholding a predicate of phenomenal shade from one while applying it to the other. In other contexts where only two things can be seen, the predicate "is the same phenomenal shade" might be correctly applied to a pair of sensory items very like a_1 and b_1 but this will not lead to problems.

This last point raises the question of whether this solution is not just a version of (3): the change of aspect suggestion. Is the observable difference between b_1 and a_1 which justifies the application of a shade predicate to one but not the other really a difference in how they ***appear***? If it is not, and this line of argument is distinct from (3), then the following simple objection arises: the difference between a_1 and b_1 in the context being merely a difference in how they compare with a third item, it should not affect a predicate designed just to describe how they appear when compared with one another. Or, to put the objection more simply, it just doesn't seem possible to deny that b_1 is indiscernible in apparent shade of colour from a_1. They look the same. So "is the same phenomenal shade as a_1" should apply to b_1. Of course the same argument applies to b_1 and c_1. We shall investigate this objection in section 8.4.

5) It might be argued that sense data have only vague properties. It is an indeterminate matter whether b_1 is a_1's shade or c_1's shade, just as it is an indeterminate matter how many leaves I see when I look at the tree outside the window. In the latter case I just see many leaves. We must simply accept the fact that perceptions can be more or less definite or determinate in this way.

We might doubt, however, that perceptions of colours can be indeterminate in the same way as perceptions of sizes and numbers of things. If we are aware of a colour it must, it seems, be some distinct, determinate colour, rather than a determinable which abstracts from or glosses over alternative possibilities. There is also the concern raised in chapter 1 about whether it makes sense to suppose any existing thing could be vague. Finally, it is not even clear that this is a solution to the problem for it is not clear that it provides grounds for rejecting (iv). If b_1 is indeterminate in shade between the shade of a_1 and that of c_1, and this does *not* mean it is intermediate in shade between the two, then it is not clear that we can refuse to apply labels for both shades to it.

6) It might be claimed that the inference from the three premisses to the conclusion (iv) is invalid due to intentionality in the language of appearances. The inference fails because the context "...appears to O to be..." is referentially opaque. So we cannot conclude from

(i) b appears to O to be the same shade as a

and

(ii) b appears to O to be the same shade as c

and

(iii) a and c appear to O to be distinct shades

that

(iv) b appears to O to be two distinct shades.

In the same way we cannot conclude from the truth of "Tom believes George is a spy" and "George is the Prime Minister's press secretary"to the truth of "Tom believes the Prime Minister's press secretary is a spy".

There is a large difference between these two inferences however, for the latter does not seem valid even in the special situation in which Tom knows of George's relation to the Prime Minister. He may not have put together the relevant bits of his knowledge. But where a, b and c are presented in the one visual context, it is hard to see how the observer can avoid putting together these various appearances. There is an air of paradox then about the above three premisses, even without the conclusion (iv). There is a puzzle about how (i), (ii) and (iii) can possibly be true at the same time.

So although it may be correct to reject the inference from (i), (ii) and (iii) to (iv), the problem cannot be completely resolved in this way. Also it is hard to see how this could solve other versions of the paradox, involving explicit mention of phenomenal properties. Taking a_1, b_1 and c_1 to refer to sensa, we could restate the paradox in the following way:

(i') a_1 is indiscernable from b_1 in phenomenal shade.

(ii') b_1 is indiscernable from c_1 in phenomenal shade.

(iii') a_1 and c_1 are discernably different in phenomenal shade.

(iv') if any two things are indiscernable in phenomenal shade they are the same phenomenal shade, and if any two things are discernably different in shade they are not the same phenomenal shade

(v') b_1 is the same phenomenal shade as two things which are different phenomenal shades.

It is unclear how the claimed intentionality in the language of appearances could enable us to avoid this dilemma.

One conclusion which may be drawn from this brief discussion is that the difficulties are not to be located solely in the language of appearances and neither are they to be eliminated simply by rejecting sense data. They might be solved, however, by adopting more than one of the above suggestions and showing how they are integrated into an adequate account of perception. We shall attempt no more than a sketch of such a solution here and try to show how it fits a certain range of theories of perception.

8.2 Phenomenal Qualities and Observational Predicates

We mentioned earlier Dummett's response to the above paradox and some problems with it. He thinks that the problem can only be resolved by denying that there are any phenomenal qualities, at least in the sense in which "phenomenal" has usually been understood. There is a refined notion of phenomenal qualities which cannot be used to generate the paradoxical argument (i) - (iv) but according to Dummett qualities meeting this definition are not properly phenomenal ones. So the paradox shows that genuine phenomenal qualities, as these have been traditionally understood, cannot exist. The refined notion Dummett discusses is Goodman's[61]. Two qualia *match*, according to Goodman's definition, just if there is no noticeable difference between them.

---

61 Goodman [1] Ch. IX

It does not follow from this that the qualia are identical. Qualia are identical if and only if they match all the same qualia. So premisses (i), (ii) and (iii) of the argument in the previous section, taken as concerning qualia, and not material objects, state resepectively that a_1 and b_1 match, b_1 and c_1 match, and a_1 and c_1 do not match. Nothing paradoxical follows from this. The matching of a pair of qualia does not mean that there is some shade that they both are. There may be some further qualia matching one but not the other.

Qualia are, of course, supposed to capture the notion of phenomenal qualities. So according to Goodman the mistake in the perceptual puzzle argument of the previous section is in assuming that because a_1 and b_1 match there is a phenomenal shade, S_a, that they both have and similarly, that b_1's match with c_1 means that both of them are the same phenomenal shade S_c. (This is a version of solution (2) of the last section.) Since a_1 and b_1 do not match all the same things they are not the same phenomenal colour in Goodman's sense. We must resist the tendency, wantonly indulged in the previous section, to immediately reify the way things appear to observers.

The objections to Goodman's notion of transitive matching as an identity criterion for phenomenal shades are well known. The notion of a phenomenal shade is supposed to capture the content of a perceiver's immediate experience and so cannot contain anything of which the perceiver is not sensorily aware. But we would not be able to judge just by looking at a pair of things or comparing them with any finite sample of objects that they were the same phenomenal shade in Goodman's sense. No matter how many objects known to be indistinguishable in shade from the one are checked and found to be indistinguishable from the other also, we could not exclude the possiblity that there exists, somewhere in the universe, a further object matching one but not the other.

It is this problem which leads Dummett to the following conclusions about Goodman's account[62]:

> In fact, we see quite generally that, within any dimension along which we can discriminate by observation at all, and within which nondiscriminable difference is non-transitive (as it surely always is), the phenomenal qualities are simply going to reflect

---

62 Dummett [1] p.323

> the distinct physical qualities, irrespective of the capacities of the observer to discriminate between them. There is, of course, nothing wrong with the definition of 'phenomenal quality' which yields this result, considered merely as a definition: but what it defines is surely not anything which we have ever taken a phenomenal quality to be.

So although Goodman's way out of the paradox might appear to be some kind of improvement on the bare statement of solution (2) above, in that the hidden properties of the sense data are all ones of which observers could become aware, it seems unsatisfactory as an account of phenomenal qualities.

There is a worse problem for the account than the one Dummett mentions. At first it appears that we may say that S_a and S_c are phenomenal shades in Goodman's permitted sense of the word and label a_1's phenomenal shade "S_a", and c_1's phenomenal shade "S_c".

For Goodman is at pains to point out (in an attempt to dismiss the oddity of calling these shades "phenomenal") that what phenomenal shades things are does depend on appearances, though in a more complex way than we might have thought. For things to be the same phenomenal shade they must not only match each other, but everything matched by one must be matched by the other also. So we have to conclude that b_1 is neither S_a or S_c, but some other phenomenal shade distinct from both of these. But S_a was defined into existence as *the shade a_1 appears to be*. If there is such a shade it is tempting to say that it is also the shade b_1 appears to be, since they look the same in shade. Since b_1 appears to be the same shade as a_1, it is also *the shade a_1 appears to be: ie. S_a*. Since this cannot be so, by the above argument it seems that S_a and S_c cannot be phenomenal shades. That is, if phenomenal shades exist they are never the shades things appear to be. For there cannot be any such shades as the shades things appear to be. If there were a_1 and b_1 would be the same shade.

If phenomenal shades are never the shades things appear to be, then they are never seen. They are quite different from the appearances things present to us. But if this is so they cannot be defined in terms of transitive matching in the way Goodman wants. Qualia were supposed to match when we could notice no difference between them, but it seems now that qualia will never be available to be checked for this.Since the phenomenal qualities of observers' sensory contents must be ones of which those observers are fully aware, the paradox is still with us. b_1 cannot be a third phenomenal shade distinct from S_a and S_c. For as argued above, the mere rejection of sense data does not seem to completely remove the problem. It would appear to arise wherever predicates are highly observational in Wright's sense and there seems to be no good reason to suppose that such predicates are satisfied only by phenomenal qualities. A predicate is purely observational in Wright's sense just if its application is standardly decided just on the basis of unaided human observation, and there seems to be no reason why there may not, as a matter of fact, be predicates which operate in this way and which are satisfied by non-phenomenal qualities of things. The predicate "red" might, for example, apply to some material object or its surfaces, but apply in such a way that the judgement of a suitably positioned competent observer upon its application to that object could not be overridden. (The judgements of different competent observers may clash however, and this is to be expected where highly observational predicates are being applied.)

8.3 Change of Aspect

An unchanging material object may impress observers differently at different moments in virtue of some single consistent set of physical qualities which it has. It may take a comparison with other objects which differ from one another to bring out these aspects of the object's appearance. This possibility might be exploited to solve the paradox by supposing that at least one of the triad alters in appearance as it is compared with the other two. Either a looks different when compared with b from the way it looks when compared with c, or b looks different when compared with a and with c, or c alters subtly in appearance between the comparison with a and with b. More than one of these things might happen, but we shall suppose that only b alters in appearance as an observer compares the three items. So at one moment, when the observer compares b with a, it is shade S_a, and at the next, when they compare it with c it is shade S_c. Jackson argues for this solution in the following way:[63]

> ...the suggestion that A might look to be the same colour as B, B might look to be the same colour as

63 Jackson [1] p.114

> C, while A looks to be a different colour from c, *to one and the same person at one and the same time,* is inconsistent. As A and C *ex hypothesi* look to be different colours, looking to be the same colour as A will be distinct from looking to be the same colour as C; therefore the suggestion involves one object, B, looking to have two different colours at the same time to the same person, which is impossible"

The observer can, of course, see all three things at once. When this occurs they will see that the first is a discernably different shade from the third. How will the middle item look? Presumably, on this view it should sometimes look indistinguishable in shade from A and sometimes indistinguishable in shade from C. What the observer cannot do is see it both ways at once, for that would necessarily involve its appearing to be two distinct shades at the same time. This way of dealing with the paradox assimilates it to other perceptual puzzle cases, such as Wittgenstein's duck/rabbit, some of Escher's drawings, Necker cubes and certain photographs of the moon in which the craters can alternately look concave and convex. One thing presents different incompatible appearances to an observer at different moments.

This suggestion also appears to provide a straightforward solution to the Sorites difficulties discussed in the previous chapters. It might take the form of a causal hypothesis designed to explain the tendency of observers to draw sharp limits to the application of any observational predicate to members of a series. The phenomenal series will not look perfectly continuous: at crucial moments one thing will appear different from one of its neighbours. But as the Sorites argument depends upon the assumption of continuity in appearances this suggestion wuld also provide the materials for a solution to the paradox itself in the general form discussed above. If S_{i-1} appears to be red at the moment t at which it is judged that S_i is indiscernable in colour from it, then S_1 must be judged to be red also; but if at some later time, t', S_i appears indiscernible in shade from something else, S_{i+1}, which does not look red, then we must conclude that S_i appears differently at these two times. We will no longer be entitled to use the conclusion, established at t, that S_i is red as a premiss for the next stage of the Sorities argument. If our only grounds for thinking it is red is its indiscernability from S_{i-1}, and those grounds are demolished when it is compared with S_{i+1}, the argument cannot get going. So the argument fails by default: at each stage we lose the grounds we had for the conclusion of the previous stage. At each stage we are entitled to detach the conclusion about the colour of the right hand member of the pair being compared, but at the next stage, when this one is compared with a further object we may be perfectly entitled to reject our earlier conclusion about its colour for it now looks different.

Though this does not seem impossible as an account of what actually might happen, it is worth stressing how odd it would be. For it seems to involve supposing that the appearance of perfect continuity in a Sorites series has to vanish whenever we look hard enough. Related illusions are not unknown: there is a phenomenon known as the end effect which consists in a difference in the appearance with respect to brightness or saturation between two physically identical coloured patches. One is the last in a series which varies gradually with respect to one of these visual variables (brightness or saturation) while the other physically identical patch is embedded in a series and is followed by further gradually varying coloured patches. In the case of series which varies with respect to saturation, the end member of the one series will look more saturated than its physically identical counterpart in the other series which is followed by more patches.[64] Retinal adaptation also causes variation in appearances with respect to hue when an object is placed on different contrasting backgrounds.

But these effects are evident and easily tested, like the alterations in the other perceptual puzzle cases mentioned above. The posited switch in appearance of b as it is compared with each of its neighbours goes unnoticed. The appearance of b as it is compared with a <u>is</u> indiscernable from the appearance of b as compared with c. b looks just the same to us when seen as b-next-to-a and when seen as b-next-to-c for we have no impression of its altering in shade. And when we look at all three in the one visual context we are not able to discriminate the shade of b from that of a or from that of c. Since there is no impression of alteration, it seems we must conclude that it is indiscriminable in shade from a and from c at the same moment which is what the argument says cannot be the case. A difference in appearances which does not appear is surely not a difference in appearances at all.

---

64 Committee on Colorimetry Optical Society of America [1] p.120

Finally, even if it can be argued that there are two sensory items, b_1 and b_2 corresponding to b seen together with a and with c, these two are surely indiscernable in shade so far as observers are concerned. So exactly the same problem arises again. Each member of the phenomenal series

$$a_1 \ b_1 \ b_2 \ c_1$$

is indiscernible from each of its immediate neighbours. So b_1 must be the same shade as a_1, since these two are indiscernible, and b_2 must be c_1's shade. But b_1 and b_2 must be the same shade also, being indiscernible from one another. Therefore one or other (or both) of them must be two shades of colour at the same time.

The last is not a possibility. As we argued earlier, rejecting the view that there are sense data will not entirely solve the problem: only an theory of perception which makes sense of the facts can do that. In the last section we shall sketch the outlines of a theory (or range of theories) which could provide a positive solution.

8.4 Tolerance and Observationality

The argument of the previous chapters could provide no grounds for rejecting the second version of the paradoxical argument outlined above ((i') - (v')). For if there are predicates which are purely observational in Wright's sense of being applied just on the basis of unaided sense perception and which are satisfied by a phenomenal properties they will be strictly tolerant. If there is available a phenomenal shade predicate, S_a, which applies to a_1, then it applies to b_1 also where these two are indisernible in shade. There is no room to add the proviso "so long as there are no other differences between the two" for S_a is just a predicate designed to apply to things which are judged to be the same phenomenal shade as a_1. Where the two are indiscernible, they must be the same phenomenal shade. In this case the arguments of earlier chapters against the Sorites do not apply, for these consisted in arguments for loose tolerance rules rather than strict tolerance rules and the relevance, where such rules operated, of discernible relational differences between the indiscernible items.

On the other hand, there are good grounds for supposing that if highly observational predicates are not satisfied by phenomenal properties, or not applied solely on the grounds of how things appear to an observer, they will not be strictly tolerant. Though predicates tied to phenomenal properties (such as S_a) would be strictly tolerant, (and so where such a predicate applied to one of an indiscernible pair it would have to apply to the other also), non-phenomenal observational predicates must be governed by loose rules. And odinary predicates, though highly observational in some instances, are not purely observational. Therefore they are governed by loose rules.

One reason why such ordinary predicates are not purely observational has to do with the public availability of the objects to which they are applied. Because they can be observed by different people, and checked over again by the same observer at different times, one observer's inability to detect any difference between two things on one occasion may be insufficient grounds for applying the same predicate to both. There are plenty of other odd circumstances, apart from those under discussion involving non-transitive matching, where someone might be justified in applying an ordinary observational predicate to one object but not another, even though they can discern no relevant difference between them by simple comparison on that occasion. An observer might know that one is some particular shade, and be unable to discern any difference between it and some other object in the available lighting, but know that this lighting is inadequate or deceptive in some way: alternatively they might know that their powers of discrimination of colours are less acute than the average, or that their discriminatory abilities are temporarily reduced due to drugs of some kind. In such circumstances they will not want to conclude that the two are the same shade, despite their inability to discern a difference. No such grounds could exist in the case of predicates which were purely observational, were there any.

Since such circumstances could always arise ordinary predicates, no matter how highly observational, will be governed by loose rules. Loose rules contain a *ceteris paribus* clause which allows for the consistent application of the predicate to one but not another of a pair of things judged indiscernible when compared just with one another by some observer. An observer may be justified in deciding on the basis of appearances that on balance an object does not deserve a predicate, even though it is indiscernible from some other things which do deserve it. The original dilemma ((i) - (iv)) of section 1 may then be dealt with in the following way. Suppose S_1 and S_2 are two shade predicates applicable to publicly observable objects. Most observers are agreed that a is S_1 and c is S_2, and a is just discernibly different in shade from c. In some contexts an observer who would apply the predicate S_1 to a will be happy to apply it to b also. But where a, b and c are juxtaposed in such a way that the observer can see that a and c are different shades, a predicate applied to a need not be applied to b also. b's appearance, overall, in such a context is such as to justify withholding either S_1 or S_2. Given these visual clues, the observer is justified in refusing to conclude that b is the same publicly observable shade as either a or c.

8.5 Vagueness in Perception

How a thing looks to us in respect of some feature such as shade of colour is not a simple uni-dimensional presentation which can be abstracted from other features of its appearance and from how it looks by comparison with other things. This conclusion - that there is some structure to "bare" appearances of publicly available objects - may of course be backed up by evidence from introspection and psychological experiment. One consequence of the complexity of appearances is that there is a measure of inconsistency about perceptual language. What is judged to be shade S_1 in one context where there are no other things available for comparison may not be judged to be so in another context where there are other objects available for comparison. This much inconsistency in our descriptions of the world can be argued to be a consequence of the looseness of fit of observational language.

Two interpretations of this view seem possible. It might be held that comparisons with other things ***merely provide criteria for determining whether the same shade predicate applies to both of a pair of things*** or else, that where a suitable third thing is available for comparison, ***two things which would otherwise look indiscernible in shade actually come to look just noticeably different in that respect***. Our reasons for rejecting the second interpretation will be clear from section 8.3. But what may not be clear is just what the effects of comparison with c can be if it is not a matter of seeing b as discernibly different from a. That is, it may be unclear what the first alternative comes to.

We noted above that the unacceptable solution (3) assimilated our puzzle case to a certain class of perceptual illusions where an unchanged object presented different appearances to an observer from moment to moment. Our perceptual puzzle seems to differ from at least some of these, such as the moon crater photographs, in that in the latter case the one appearance (craters concave) appears to block the other (craters convex) appearance. But where the three objects, a, b and c, are laid out in the one visual context, there is no comparable switch in the way b appears from moment to moment.[65] At least none has been noted in the rellevant literature. Observers report that while b looks no different in shade from a and from c, a and c do look discernibly different in shade. The one appearance does not block the other. The comparison of b with each of the others does have some effect however: when b is compared with the further object, c, as well as with a, the observer notices a certain aspect of b's appearance which is not evident when just a and b are seen together. This aspect of its appearance, which is brought out by the comparison with c, does not prevent the observer from also noticing the apparent resemblance to a. While it does seem to be possible for someone to notice that b is indiscernible in shade from both and c while at the same time noticing that a and c are just discernibly different in shade, such an observer does not see b as being two shades of colour at the same time. What is needed now is an account of perception which makes this feat possible.

The only way this perceptual feat would seem to be possible is for the perception of b, throughout the experience, to be perfectly indeterminate as between being a perception of something of a's shade or of something of c's shade. "Indeterminate" here does not mean "intermediate": the assumption is that the observer is incapable of discriminating shades between these two. What is meant here by indeterminacy in perception is similar to Quine's notion of indeterminacy in meaning. Just as there is no fact of the matter as to whether the field linguist's subject means "set of undetached rabbit parts" or "instance of the universal: rabbithood" by their utterance of "Gavagai!", so there is no fact of the matter as to whether our observer perceives b as one shade or the other. It is possible to recognize in a single perception the potential for leading in different visual directions.

One objection raised at the start to this way out was that it seems that when we observe something red we see that it is some determinate specific shade of red. Perception may be indeterminate when it involves not noticing detail (as it is in the case when we see that there is some large number of leaves on a tree, but do not see how many there are, but this is not a case of

---

65 It is often claimed that an observer cannot discern at the same moment both the ducklike aspect of Wittgenstein's drawing and the rabbitlike one. I am not sure that this claim is correct. Some of the illusions of this class appear to be closer to our puzzle case than others.

noticing detail. It seems wrong, however, to suppose that perception of colour is always determinate in this way. Suppose that immediately after viewing a red cloth we are shown two other similar red things and asked to say whether the cloth matched one or the other or neither. We may say, "I didn't notice exactly what shade it was" or, "I can't remember its shade well enough to tell". If the objection held, we could never give the first of these replies. It would always be false to say that we did not see exactly what shade a thing is, if we notice it at all. Since the first of these replies seems a reasonable one, and distinct from the second, the objection cannot hold.

If we take this way out of the paradox should we also say that the argument from (i) to (iv) is fallacious and that one cannot conclude from the three premisses that b appears to any observer to be two distinct shades at the same time? It was suggested before that where b is indeterminate in shade some grounds would have to be given refusing to apply both shade predicates to it. The connexion between indefiniteness in perception and intentionality in the language of sensation and observation (as noted for instance by Anscombe)[66] may provide such a ground. For this is a source of failures of inferences in other cases. What is seen or looked for under a relatively unspecific or indefinite description may be identical with something fitting a relatively specific description unknown to the perceiver. So it may be true that

John is looking for the person in charge

but not true that he is looking for Mary, even though (unknown to John) she is that person. Indeterminacy in thought or perception of an object makes it possible that not every true description of the object is one under which it is seen or thought of. There does appear to be a kind of vagueness involved in indeterminate descriptions of what is perceived in such cases, but it is related to the ordinary conception of vagueness as indefiniteness described in section 1.3, rather than vagueness of the borderline case sort which we are investigating here.

There is a range of theories of perception which might accommodate this feature and so allow for a complete resolution of the paradox. It has been suggested[67] that a large part of perceiving consists in arriving at judgements upon objects.

---

66 See, for instance Anscombe in [1]

67 See, for example Craig [1]

Judgements may be more or less definite: one thing may be taken to be at least as large as another without there being any commitment to either of the exclusive alternatives of their being equal or unequal in size. This kind of view would allow for the possiblity that our perception of the colour b in the triad discussed above is indeterminate as between a judgement of it as a's shade or as c's shade. A similar view is suggested by the psychologist R.L. Gregory[68], who takes perceiving to consist in the forming of hypotheses about the world. Hypotheses are often best left indefinite in order to be refined as further evidence appears or the requirements they must meet become clearer.

Another kind of view of perception preferred by many psychologists takes it to consist in the picking up of information from the world. The pattern of ambient light reflected from objects conveys information determined by their position and relation to one another. Gibson's original account[69] of the way in which the structure of the optical array determines perception of the world makes it clear that the information conveyed may be more or less specific. The optical information picked up need only be specific enough to ensure a construction of objects adequate for the purposes human and animal perception has evolved to meet.

Neisser, another psychologist, develops Gibson's views in a way which allows for a positive contribution on the part of the perceiver. His theory makes it possible to account for the role of expectations and stored information in directing perception and so permits an explanation of why some aspects of things are noticed rather than others. A single object may even offer contradictory information, he claims, in that it may support two "perceptual cycles" of exploration and construction which cannot be integrated.[70] He stresses that these are not constructions of mental images appearing in consciousness.

> The information picked up in vision is necessarily optical, consisting of patterns in the light over space and time. But optical information can specify objects and events at various levels of abstraction and

68 See Gregory [1]

69 see Gibson [1]

70 Neisser [1] p.44

> meaning, and a schema organized on one level need not be sensitive to the others.[71]

Provided that some account of perception within this range is acceptable, it seems that the paradox may be resolved. It is, as argued above, a problem with a number of dimensions and the solution offered in 8.4 seems necessary to resolve those which surface as questions about the coherence of perceptual language. This solution would be consistent with any of the theories of perception mentioned in this section. We have argued that the refusal to project the application of an observational predicate past a certain point is justified on the basis of what is perceived, and any of these accounts of the nature of perception can provide further details of the nature of this justification.

---

71 Neisser [1] p.21

Chapter 9

CONCLUSIONS

9.1 The Induction Step and Continua in Nature

We arrived in earlier chapters at the conclusions that the Sorites is not an insoluble paradox and the vagueness of observational predicates is not a source of radical incoherence in natural language. The solution offered in chapter 6 does not require the rejection of established principles of reasoning or the overhaul of semantic theory. We may keep our intuitions concerning the validity of the reasoning involved in Sorites arguments and the tolerance of observational predicates. For the source of the problem, on this view, is to be found not in the logical principles used to establish the paradoxical conclusions but rather in the formulation of tolerance principles as strict rather than loose rules and in assumptions about the series on which the reasoning is based.

We saw in section 4.4 that all versions of Sorites reasoning assumed the existence of a series of things ordered with respect to their possession of features relevant to the application of some predicate. The series must be one in which the predicate clearly applied at one end but not the other and in which the variation in relevant properties was so gradual that no sharp differences between members in any of these respects could be detected by casual observation. One conclusion we might now draw from our argument of the previous chapters is that this assumption about the existence of such series is false. It turns out, when the assumption is investigated in more detail, that suitable series would have to have two incompatible features: they would have to exhibit (apparent) perfect continuity in every respect relevant to the application of the predicate to be projected and also non-transitive indiscernibility from member to member in all those respects. These features are incompatible, since non-transitive indiscernibility creates evident *differences* from member to member in a respect relevant to the application of the predicate. Unless the series exhibited non-transitive indiscernibility that predicate could not apply at one end but not the other.

What conclusion should be drawn about the validity of the induction step of the argument? Most solutions to the Paradox (including the fuzzy logics and the supervaluation approach) involve rejecting it as false (or at least as slightly less than true) but this is never felt to be a satisfactory way out. It needs at least to be reconciled with those intuitions about the vagueness of observational predicates which lead us to suppose that where such a predicate applies to one member of an apparently continuous series it must also apply to the next. Dissatisfaction with this solution, consisting just of the of rejection of the induction step, is brought into focus by Wright's arguments for the tolerance of observational predicates. To reject the induction step seems to involve denying that these predicates are vague in Frege's sense of lacking sharp boundaries to their application. But, as we saw in earlier chapters, there is plenty of evidence that they are vague in just this sense.

The solution suggested above provides a way around these difficulties. For the induction step may be taken as a claim about series of a certain kind and there can be no series of that kind. If there were (as the Sorites arguments leads us to assume), it would, of course, be true that a predicate which applies to any arbitrary member will apply to its successor also, for this is true of any series which has the first of these two characteristics. Where there is perfect indiscernibility in every observable respect from member to member an observational predicate which applies to an arbitrarily chosen member of the series will apply to its successor also. There are, of course, series of this sort, but they are ones in which an observational predicate which applies at one end applies at the other also. Any actual series which varies throughout in some relevant observable respect so that the predicate is true at one end but not the other will also be discontinuous in some relevant observable respect.

This is not to say that there are no continua in nature. Series which actually vary will be continuous in some respects but not others, and the fact that there may be continuities in certain dimensions of appearance and discontinuities in others provides grounds for rejecting strict tolerance rules. Such rules would be inappropriate for creatures with our perceptual limitations for they would force us to project a predicate wherever we are unable to discern a difference in some dimension. Only loose rules could allow us to cope with unforeseen complexities and continuities in nature, since these rules allow us options when confronted with difficult or borderline cases. Rules for the application of observational terms must allow scope for inductive judgement, expertise and stipulative decisions. No strict, mechanically applicable principles can allow this scope and flexibility.

It seems then that we might locate the source of the paradox in either of two places: we may say either that the induction step is true as a claim about series of a certain kind but there are no series of the kind the argument assumes, or we may say that the induction step is false for all actual series which exhibit variation in the relevant respects. There is no great difference between these conclusions but the first seems less misleading since it locates the source of the trouble in the Sorites reasoning.

9.2 The Existence of Fregean Vagueness

We argued earlier that the Sorites Paradox only arises where there is vagueness of the kind Frege characterizes. Where a term is vague in this sense, boundaries cannot be drawn to delimit the scope of its correct application. Various solutions to the Sorites have been rejected along the way on the grounds that they consisted merely of ignoring or stipulating away the existence of vagueness of this kind. The question which now arises is whether, in solving the Paradox, we have merely eliminated Fregean vagueness and so failed to come to terms with the problem in the form in which it is presented by Dummett and Wright. The suspicion that this might be so could arise because we have argued that where any real series varies in respects relevant to the application of an observational predicate an observer will be justified in refusing to apply that predicate past some point. Observers are entitled on the basis of what they observe to judge that one member deserves the predicate but the next does not. This amounts, it seems, to saying that they are permitted to draw sharp boundaries to the application of observational predicates. It would seem to follow that such predicates could not be vague in the sense with which we have been concerned, the sense in which there are no sharp limits to the scope of application of a vague predicate. Where a predicate is vague its applicability fades off imperceptibly; vagueness of this sort does not appear to be compatible with the drawing of sharp boundaries.

This conclusion does not follow however. An observer who draws a sharp limit to the application of an observational predicate in one context is not thereby bound to draw the line at the same point when confronted with the same series over again in another context. And different observers will draw the line at different points in a single context. Since they are equally justified on the basis of appearance, it seems the account of what observers do and why is perfectly compatible with the view that observational predicates lack sharp boundaries. This raises some complex issues which are to be discussed in the next section.

9.3 Constraints on Observer and Theorist

It is not entirely clear on Frege's characterization of vagueness or on Dummett's or Wright's discussions of the problem ***who*** is not permitted by the vagueness of observational predicates to draw sharp limits at any point to their application. It seems that Dummett's main concern is with the semantic theorist. His argument about vagueness in language seems designed to show that no correct account of a vague language can represent its observational predicates as having sharply delimited boundaries. Such a language could not be used by creatures with our perceptual limitations. Therefore, any adequate semantic account of a natural language must represent its observational predicates as vague in the Fregean sense.

Wright's arguments, on the other hand, concern the ordinary users of the language and are clearly intended to show that if they are to abide by the rules of sense that they have adopted as governing observational predicates, they cannot at any point draw sharp limits to the scope of observational predicates. Both can agree with Frege that lack of sharp boundaries is an essential feature of the sense of observational predicates, but Wright's thesis, at least, is stronger than this. He claims, not just that the rules for the application of an observational predicate fail to provide ordinary users with sharp criteria delimiting their scope, but that the sense the users have attached to those predicates *does not permit them* ever to draw limits in practice to their scope.

This stronger thesis is surely implausible. If the rules fail to determine how to treat some borderline case they must leave an individual free to choose. Where a decision matters they may go one way or the other; if it does not matter they will not decide at all. We saw in early sections that there is general acceptance of a range of divergent applications of vague predicates and indifference as to how the matter is settled where cases are genuinely borderline.

The strong thesis is not just implausible: Wright's arguments clearly fail to establish its truth. One argument was that the point of applying observational predicates was to characterize things according to the way they appear to a casual glance. Predicates with sharp limits to their scope could not be used in this way. If sharply defined limits were part of the meaning of observational predicates we would have to perform impossible feats of memory to apply them correctly and ostensive training in their use would not be possible. But these arguments only show that sharp limits are not part of the meaning of observational predicates. No specific limits to the application of such predicates are understood as being laid down in advance when their meaning is grasped. These arguments support only the weaker claim that the sense of observational predicates does not serve to specify precisely where the boundaries of application are to be drawn, not the strong thesis that no boundaries are ever to be drawn.

9.4 Fregean Vagueness, Loose Tolerance Rules and Undecidability

Our adoption of loose rather than strict tolerance rules helps to resolve the appearance of conflict between the refusal on the part of an individual in a context to apply predicates beyond a certain point, and the vagueness of those predicates. Since the rules adopted by individuals as governing their application of observational predicates are loose rules and cannot be further refined, they determine the limits of the application of the predicates only roughly. There is no spelling out the sense of the predicates in more detail so as to produce rules which give more detailed instructions about where to draw the line. But it is a fact about the perceptual and linguistic capacities of normal human beings that the adoption of rules of this rough sort, together with suitable training, is sufficient to guarantee a large amount of consistency in the use of the predicate. Decisions about the limits of application of predicates of this sort are not arbitrary; neither are they completely determined in specific detail by the rules of sense for the predicates. The rules suffice to justify the decisions made but, since they are vague (in the ordinary sense of failing to decide between distinct options), they may be used to justify conflicting decisions.

We have argued that observational predicates fit the world only loosely, that there is a certain amount of slack in their application conditions which is to be taken up by individual judgement and stipulation. This view fits the linguistic evidence, since one competent observer may apply an observational predicate to an object and another refuse to do so without its being concluded that either is mistaken about the facts or in their grasp of the concepts involved. Judgements made at different times by a single observer are often inconsistent in the same way. Since this is so, it must be an indeterminate matter whether or not some things belong in the extension of observational predicates. Then, if the boundaries of application of these predicates may be drawn in various places with no fact of the matter as to which is the best, the predicate would seem to be vague in the sense with which we began. The limits of its application are unclear, for it is an indeterminate matter which of these alternative ways of drawing them is correct. We can conclude that the picture of the application of the vague predicate fading away imperceptibly is a correct picture of the vagueness of predicates of the communal language.

Vagueness of this sort is compatible with the existence of rough boundaries - hazy limits to the scope of application of vague observational predicates. A knowledge of these rough limits will be built into the rules grasped by the competent user of the language for the application of the predicates. These rules surely do not dictate that there are no limits to be drawn: they leave users of the language free to decide within some roughly defined zone where they will cease to apply the predicate. Our arguments of earlier chapters showed that these rules cannot be further refined and no more thorough investigation of the linguistic data will uncover sharp limits to the range of acceptable boundaries.

So our arguments are compatible with the weaker thesis that the rules of sense of observational predicates are not such as to determine exactly where their boundaries are to be drawn. If the rules did determine this precisely, competent users of the language would apply the predicates consistently or where they diverged, regard unknown facts of the matter as determining that one or the other application was correct. But ordinary understanding of the sense of words such as "red" is not sufficient to say where, in general, the boundaries of its application will be drawn by all users, or by a majority of users. This is just to say it is vague in our original sense. The occasional decisions on borderline cases made by individuals do not conflict with the vagueness in the meanings of the predicates they use: rather the diversity in the range of acceptable responses in such situations provides part of the evidence for the claim that this vagueness exists. So it does not follow from Wright's arguments or, more generally, from the conception of the Fregean vagueness of observational predicates that ordinary users of the language are committed by rules of sense which they may be seen as having implicitly adopted to a refusal in practice to draw limits anywhere to the scope of application of those predicates. It does follow from Wright's and Dummett's arguments that the rules of sense for observational predicates cannot, in general, determine sharp limits to the extension of those predicates.

9.5 Vagueness as a Pragmatic Phenomenon

To preserve the idea of boundaries of the extension of terms in the communal language fading away imperceptibly we must say that it cannot *in general* be true that there is some member of every series which is such that the term applies to it but not to its successor. The application of the predicate stops somewhere then, but there is no saying precisely where that point is. Since this is genuine undecidability, and not mere epistemological uncertainty, there is no truth of the matter as to which member of the series it is that is the first to which the predicate fails to apply. There is of course a last member for each individual observer in a particular context, but this choice is not fully determined by the generally agreed upon rules for the application of the predicate. Those rules neither prohibit nor determine the individual's drawing of limits where they do. A theory which allowed, as a result of the falsehood of the induction step for actual series, that there was in general some (unknown) determinate last member of each series to which the predicate applied would be a theory which failed to give an account of the vagueness of those predicates. It would solve the problems about vagueness by precisifying it away.

Our problem, then, is to see how to provide an adequate account of a vague language which does not eliminate its vagueness in this way. Where that vagueness is Fregean it seems that no precise set-theoretic model or set of such models could be adequate, since the boundaries to the application of predicates can be only roughly drawn. (This seems to be the substance of Dummett's objection in "Wang's Paradox" to supervaluation accounts.) An account of a natural language which did not ignore or eliminate its vagueness would have to differ from an account of a non-vague language. What should this difference amount to? Standard answers locate the difference in the semantics of vague languages and particularly in the rejection of Bivalence. But, as we saw in early sections of chapter 3, it is not at all clear that Bivalence does fail in the presence of vagueness. (Nor is it clear that it holds.) One surely correct, though not very informative, answer to our question is that an account of a vague language is called upon to explain more than is an account of a perfectly precise language. For, presumably, an account of a natural language should explain certain features of the linguistic behaviour of the population which uses that language. Which features are taken to need explanation depends on our interests, and where our interest is vagueness we will want an account adequate to explain the inconsistency, hesitation and uncertainty which constitute the grounds for claiming that a language is vague. Also, an account of any natural language ought to make sense of the linguistic behaviour of its users: as we saw earlier, the thesis that natural language is inconsistent is not acceptable because it fails to meet this general requirement. And so an adequate account ought to provide some means of dealing with the Sorites Paradox.

A pragmatic account of vagueness, such as that proposed by Lewis, meets both requirements. On this kind of account the difference between a vague language and a precise one consists in the relation between users and language, rather than between language and the world. Where there is no vagueness a population may be represented as speaking a single precise language; where there is vagueness speakers must be represented as alternating between members of a range of such languages. There is no difficulty on such an account of vagueness in explaining speakers' hesitation over borderline cases or the inconsistent decisions made about such objects from one speaker to the next or on the part of one speaker in different contexts. Where there is a range of distinct precise languages to choose from differing at just those points where questions about the application of vague predicates arise, individuals may be expected to dither occasionally, to be inconsistent and to differ from one another in the decisions they make about borderline objects. It is also easy to explain why we are usually unconcerned by these inconsistencies and do not bother to resolve them in ordinary circumstances. For there is no single communal language: we speak a range of languages and accept as reasonable any application of a predicate dictated by the use of a language within the cluster.

Such an account is clearly better as an explanation of the uncertainty and inconsistency characteristic of a vague language than one which takes vagueness to be a purely semantic matter. Semantic uncertainty of the kind discussed in chapter 3 may seem to offer a plausible account of the uncertainty felt by speakers confronted with a borderline case of a vague predicate, for where it is uncertain in this sense whether or not an object is to be counted as within the extension of such a predicate, speakers might be expected to feel hesitant about applying the predicate. But, if the vagueness is Fregean, there is a further uncertainty about the boundaries of the area of uncertainty and, as we saw, there appears to be no way the supervaluation theory can account for this dimension of vagueness, since it must take the admissible ways of precisifying vague predicates to be sharply delimited. The pragmatic account carries no implication that there are sharp boundaries to the limits of borderline cases. Inconsistencies are not averaged out, as in fuzzy logic accounts, but explained as variation in usage. If a population is taken to be speaking a single language which is semantically vague, it is difficult to see how individuals could be justified in drawing sharp limits to the application of predicates at different points. This is intelligible if those individuals are seen as having adopted at various times different precise languages dictating different sharp cut-off points to the application of the predicate.

On this view, the difficulties which led to the Sorites Paradox are to be located in the false account of the relation between linguistic behaviour and the communal language. It remains to be seen how well the correct account of the relation can deal with Sorites puzzles, and this will be discussed in detail in the next section. One last point we should mention here concerns the problem raised in chapter 2 about the relation between the verbal activities of a population of language users and the precise artificial languages designed to represent those activities. It is obvious now how to deal with the objection that the relation cannot be anything but explication and hence, that such precise accounts are bound to ignore vagueness. For, if vagueness is due to uncertainty in the linguistic habits of that population, it may fairly be represented by a range of precise alternative explications or precisifications: such an account does not eliminate these alternatives.

9.6 Tolerance and the Actual Language Relation

The view that the linguistic behaviour of a population is to be explained by their adoption of a cluster of similar precise languages rather than a single one leads to the following question: when does a cluster of similar precise languages count as the one actually spoken by some population? As we saw in 2.3, Lewis's answer makes use of the notion of conventions to tell the truth in particular languages of the group. This notion leaves it unclear whether or not the conventions define a sharply delimited group of languages. A dilemma of a now familiar kind might be generated at this point: if the cluster of languages is seen as sharply bounded, it may be suggested that vagueness has been eliminated; while if the boundaries to the group of languages spoken by some population are hazy, there would seem to be some possibility of reviving a version of the Sorites Paradox. The latter possibility arises if speakers of a natural language, such as English, are conceived of as speaking a cluster of precise interpreted languages which are not sharply bounded, since hazy boundaries are naturally associated with tolerance. It seems possible to imagine a series of dialects with only minor variations from one to the next ranging from central cases of English to central cases of Chinese. If any language is a member of the cluster which might reasonably be used by a speaker of English, so must the next, surely, for the difference between one and the next is so small.

To adopt the alternative solution and say that the languages of the cluster are sharply delimited and so (unknown) empirical facts determine where the boundaries lie will not provide a satisfactory way out of the problem. For it would falsify the psychological reality on which the conception of language is based. When a child grasps the meanings of terms of a natural language it does not select out any one of a range of precise languages, and neither does it sharply define the boundaries of the range of precise languages. Also, the conventions which, according to Lewis, determine which languages are actually spoken by a group are based on expectations and intentions which are bound to be hazy. They will be vague in the sense in which psychological phenomena are vague (see section 1.23) and so fail to discriminate between alternative options. So the conventions based upon them will fail to determine sharp limits to the range of languages spoken by a population. Further considerations to do with open texture and the requirements of flexibility in natural languages could also be used to argue for the view that there are only rough boundaries to the cluster of languages spoken by any given population.

The way out of this dilemma recapitulates some of the arguments of chapter 6. The precise interpreted languages spoken by a population diverge over the objects which count as borderline for each predicate and, if there is Fregean vagueness here, there are no sharp limits in each case to the class of these objects. If the arguments of previous sections are correct, this means that individuals are free to decide where to draw limits within this hazy area. Of course it is not possible to tell in advance of unexpected contingencies and unimaginable borderline cases which definite decisions are going to seem best to individuals applying these predicates. So although the limits to the range of precise languages which may be spoken by a given population must be regarded as indeterminate, there is no danger of the range spreading in such a way that the languages of one group of speakers cannot be distinguished from those of another. The linguistic behaviour of individual speakers will determine limits in practice, though the theorist has no way of specifying them in advance.

9.7 Bivalence, Vagueness and Truth

This pragmatic conception of vagueness also provides the resources to settle a dispute concerning Bivalence and vague languages which was left unresolved in chapter 3. In 3.1 we argued that the rejection of the Principle of Bivalence was satisfactory only if it was possible to shift the consequent problems up a level to be resolved by a theory of higher order vagueness. But in the final sections of the chapter we found that accounts which rejected Bivalence failed to resolve these difficulties. The main problems concerned the adequacy of accounts of the uncertainty characteristic of a vague language, an uncertainty which is not epistemological and concerned the applicability of vague predicates to their borderline cases. The trouble with rejecting Bivalence as a response to the difficulty is that the borderline cases of a predicate would then cease to be cases where its application is uncertain. Where b is a borderline case of F-hood, "Fb" would count as neither true nor false. It seems better to treat genuinely borderline objects as cases of uncertain predication. But to say that Bivalence holds and "Fb" is either true or false, even where b is a borderline case and we do not know which truth value the statement has, is (on one view of matters) to say that unknown facts decide the issue one way or the other and this seems wrong. It is wrong because it seems to imply that really there are no borderline cases. And if "Fb" is true or false then it must be one or the other so surely an omnipotent being could tell which. But since no extension of human powers could be adequate to decide the issue it seems idle to suppose there is a fact of the matter.

We preferred to say at one point that where b is a borderline case of F-hood, the relevant facts do not determine that "Fb" is something other than true or false but leave it uncertain which it is. We were concerned about the response that if it is not something other than true or false it is one or the other. Then it is either true or false, though we don't know which. The best position seemed to be one which kept Bivalence but regarded the truth value of vague statements as uncertain in the required sense. On the pragmatic approach to vagueness, we can justify this position and have things both ways. If we suppose our precise languages to be bivalent, "Fb" will be either true or false in each language but speakers may adopt different languages from one another and shift from one language to another at different times. It is the habits of language use, rather than languages themselves, which are uncertain on this view. The borderline cases of a predicate's application are those things whose exclusion or inclusion within the extension of the predicate distinguish one language from another. So b may be a borderline case even though "Fb" never counts as anything other than true or false. And though there are sharp breaks in the applicability of a predicate in each language the uncertain status of its borderline cases is respected.

It seems correct to accept Bivalence where there is vagueness, since the uncertainty associated with vagueness is often due to inconsistency. In some contexts the statement "Fred is short" may be passed off as perfectly acceptable, but in others, where more careful comparisons are being made, it might be more acceptable to say that he is not really short. The facts about Fred's actual height do not determine that one or the other is wrong, for they do not decide that one unique language is best for describing reality. Some languages may (for further pragmatic reasons to be investigated in the next section) be a more appropriate choice than others in a particular context and so it seems wrong to claim that such statements lack a truth value entirely.

To say that something is a borderline case of some predicate is, therefore, to make a remark about the likelihood that individual speakers will diverge in their decisions on the application of the predicate to it and so make inconsistent remarks about it. It is necessary to equivocate now on the question of whether the truth and falsehood predicates are vague. If the question concerns the predicates of the metalanguages of particular precise object languages, the answer is that they are not at all vague. Bivalence holds in all the languages of the cluster associated with a syntactically individuated natural language. If the question concerns the definiteness of the semantic status of every statement of the syntactically individuated language, then the answer has to be that there is uncertainty in some cases as to whether a statement is true or false and so there is vagueness. For an individual may choose either option in particular contexts. In the final section we shall discuss in detail the way in which the determination of the truth-value of vague statements depends upon features of context. In the last section and the one immediately following this we shall also look briefly at some suggestions about the sources of vagueness in natural languages.

9.8 Vagueness in Language and in Psychological Phenomena

We suggested early in chapter 1 that psychological phenomena might sometimes be vague in a sense distinct from the borderline case vagueness evident in natural languages, and that there may be a relation between the two. Borderline case vagueness of natural language predicates is also blamed upon an indefiniteness in concepts (Frege) and on a lack of determinacy in meanings (Fine). In this section we shall investigate the relations between vague psychological phenomena, meanings and borderline case vagueness in language with a view to uncovering some sources of Fregean vagueness in the latter.

On the Lewisian account we have been discussing in the last few sections, a language is a set-theoretic entity which may be investigated in abstraction from the activities of its users. A language is a function which has as its domain certain sequences of types of sounds and marks and as its range, *meanings*. Meanings are also functions: in the case of sentences they are functions from possible worlds to truth-values. Since the truth-value of a sentence depends on context (in various ways which will be discussed in the next section), its meaning may be identified with the set of possible worlds assigned to it on an occasion of its utterance. The meanings of constituents of sentences - names, predicates etc. - are also functions: functions from possible worlds to individuals (in the case of names) or to sets of individuals. The meanings of more grammatically complex constituents such as adjectives and adverbs are functions from meanings to meanings.

Language is also a rational and conventional social phenomenon: a sphere of action and communication. Lewis's account of the relation between these two conceptions of language is as follows. Marks and sounds (utterances) acquire linguistic meanings from their role in a certain system of intentions and beliefs. A person who wants to bring about a response of a certain kind in another (the kind of response being, typically, a belief or an action) will produce a certain utterance in the belief that this will achieve that goal and achieve it in part by means of the audience's recognition of their intention to bring about, by means of the utterance, that very response. So a sentence of a language L comes to mean what it does because of certain regularities in the behaviour of speakers of L and their audiences.

An adequate analysis of linguistic meaning must also provide some account of its conventional nature. The regularities in speaker/hearer behaviour are arbitrary according to Lewisin that others could have been chosen which would have served as well. They are also self-sustaining, in that their existence provides a population of speakers with reasons for further conformity. This self-sustaining mechanism works, according to Lewis, by way of commmonly held beliefs and general preferences for conformity as outlined in section 2.3.

A particular group of people are users of the same precise language when there exists among them a convention of truthfulness and trust in that language. Unlike other groups, they will form intentions and respond to utterances in accordance with this convention. Ordinarily, speakers of L will utter a declarative sentence s of L iff they believe s to be true and wish others to believe it also; on the whole L-users respond to utterances of s by coming to believe that s is the case (or at least that the utterer believes s to be the case).

Indefiniteness in propositional attitudes can produce vagueness at a number of points on this account. Linguistic meanings will not, of course, be vague on Lewis's account, but what may be called speaker meanings may be.[72] Intentions and beliefs may be indefinite in content in the way suggested in section 1.2(c) and, as a consequence, it may be uncertain which precise range of possible worlds is assigned by someone to a sentence which they are willing to assert on some occasion. The uncertainty here is not merely epistemological. There may be no fact of the matter as to what a person believes or intends by an utterance and so alternative construals of their propositional attitudes may be equally reasonable given complete knowledge of their behaviour and physical states. The same variety of indeterminacy infects the

72 See Grice [2], [3] and Schiffer [1] for alternative views of the relation between these notions.

meanings of sentence constituents. Uncertainty in the belief-inducing intention with which a speaker asserts a sentence in a particular context produces uncertainty about its truth-value. Beliefs adopted in response to utterances may be equally indefinite. Hence there will be divergent assessments of borderline cases and conflicting assignments of truth values to borderline cases on the part of different individuals in the same context, and on the part of the same individual in different contexts. Indefiniteness in the beliefs and intentions involved makes tolerance of a range of alternatives reasonable.

This uncertainty also means that the regularities which constitute linguistic conventions will not be precise, universal and totally predictable. We know only roughly what to expect of other people, how they will respond to utterances of ours, and which sets of possible worlds they associate with which sequences of types of sounds and marks. Thus alternative conventions may fit the facts of linguistic behaviour and make conflicting hypotheses concerning speakers' propositional attitudes equally reasonable. Also, a system of beliefs and desires may not comprise a fully determinate convention of truthfulness and trust in any definite language. It may be uncertain therefore which language is spoken by an individual or a group of people. An account of some further sources of this uncertainty in speaker's attitudes and of how it may sometimes be resolved by context will be given in the last two sections.

9.9 Vagueness, Precision and Context-Dependence

We have seen in earlier chapters that features of the context in which a vague sentence is uttered often serve to resolve uncertainty concerning its truth-value. Whether it is true or false that George is bald depends on where the line is drawn between those who are bald and those who are not, and various factors operate in particular contexts to determine which of a range of reasonable delineations of the boundaries applies. Where a sentence is true at any of these we may, following Lewis in [4], call it *simply true*; sentences count as *true enough* if they are true over a large enough area of this range. When a sentence counts as true enough is a vague matter. It depends on our willingness to assert and accept the sentence and this will obviously vary from context to context. Lewis singles out from among the variables which matter here the *standard of precision* operating in the context in which the sentence is uttered. A sentence such as

"France is hexagonal" which is acceptable under low standards of precision, will be rejected if standards are raised.

The context of an utterance, according to Lewis in [5], is fully determined by its location in physical space and time and in logical space (the space of possible worlds). This location determines countless further features on which its truth may depend. But its truth may also depend on shifts envisaged by speaker and audience away from the actual context of utterance: features such as time, place, world and standard of precision which may shift in the course of a conversation in response to changes in the direction and focus of interest of the discourse. These shiftable features are part of the *index* of an utterance and truth, according to Lewis, depends on both index and context. Indexical shifts are shifts away from the index of the context: the indexical features given by the actual location of the context.

It is not entirely clear how some of these indexical shifts on which truth depends actually work. Does a shift to higher standards of precision mean that fewer people count as bald *and* fewer as non-bald than would so count under lower standards? (That is, do higher standards generate more borderline cases?) Or do high standards shift the true/false boundary only without altering the size of the class of borderline cases? The former seems plausible in the case of "bald" (when we care more about precision we may discriminate more borderline cases) while the discussion of "France is hexagonal" suggests the latter consequence. While true (or at least true enough) under low standards, this sentence counts as *false* once standards are raised. What determines the standard of precision at the index of a context? Shifts in the standards in the course of a conversation are obviously determined by the interests and purposes of the participants and by presuppositions created and carried along by the shifting focus of the conversation, but exactly how do these factors operate?

Other features of context closely related to the standards of precision provide clues to the answers to these questions. Comparison with other objects available in a context often serves to resolve questions about the status of some object with respect to a vague predicate and so helps to determine the truth value of sentences about it. "d is a small nail" might have an uncertain truth value in many contexts in which there is a large range of nails of various sizes available . But in a context in which there are only two sizes of nails to be found, the same nail might count as definitely small. Our solution to the Sorites Paradox in chapter

6 suggests that even in the former context comparison with other nails just discriminably different in size may be used to resolve the question, when it must be resolved. Suppose the nails are arranged in order of length and the differences between each one and the next are too small to be discriminated without careful measurement. An observer may count d as the last of the small nails even though they can discern no difference in size between it and the next, for d may, unlike the next, look indiscernible from some clearly small nails.

The truth-value of sentences uttered in a context may be decided not just by comparison with objects available in that context. We saw in 7.6 that the appropriateness of an application of a vague predicate is also determined by remembered past applications of it in similar contexts and on unremembered effects of such applications on the speaker's perceptual judgements. Very often the participants in a conversation have a range of possible discriminations or classifications in mind which are applied to the actual objects available in the context and which determine relevant comparisons and standards of precision. Where speaker and audience have in mind the full range of possible contours of the boundaries of countries "France is hexagonal" is likely to be rejected as false (and as "too vague" in the ordinary sense distinguished in section 1.3) while if, for some reason, they are thinking just of a restricted range of simple geometric shapes (including, say, just triangles, squares, circles and hexagons) the sentence will be perfectly acceptable. With some other less restricted range of classifications in the background the sentence may be uncertain in truth value.

In the final section we shall investigate further the notion of a classification range with a view to throwing some light on the questions raised earlier in this section and also on a puzzle remaining from chapter 1 section 1.3 concerning the relation between the borderline case conception of vagueness and the ordinary notion of vagueness as indefiniteness.

9.10 Classification Ranges

We shall take a classification range to be a co-ordinate of the index of an utterance which is determined by the states of mind of the participants in a conversation. The wider the range, the more discriminations it permits. The more inclusive the ways contemplated of dividing up the field of interest of the discourse, the wider the range of possible contrasts. Most normal conversational contexts set a natural classification range, thus determining that feature of the index of the context. For example vagueness of the ordinary kind is often a result of deliberate violations of the standards set by natural classification ranges. Prospective passengers asking about the time of a train's departure will often be contemplating a classification range which enables discriminations between minutes as well as hours. To be told the train will be departing sometime soon will be unsatisfactory, since it is appropriate only against a narrower classification range enabling discriminations only of 'sooner' rather than 'later'.

It appears then that the satisfactoriness of a conversational contribution depends on there being a match both between the classification range the speaker and audience have in mind, and between these and the relevant discriminations they are interested in making, or able to make, in the context. Accusations of vagueness often involve divergences in the classification range accepted by speaker and audience or between the range they accept and the range of discriminations possible in the context. The exchange, "Where did you go?" "Out." is unsatisfactory for the former reason to one participant because they have in mind a range of options the other insists on ignoring. The dimensions of vagueness which have to do with lack of specificity and uninformativeness fit into the overall picture here. The connexion between vagueness and lack of clarity due to glossing over distinguishable options may also be a result of the choice of classification ranges which are ill-matched to the context. Where an audience is able to make a discrimination at a conceptual level which is not permitted by the classification range adopted by the speaker, they are likely to reject the speaker's utterance as too vague. This technique of criticism may be abused however. (See Lewis's discussion of Unger's flatter-than-flat argument in [4], p.182).

In general, a natural classification range is set by the context, and acceptance of it appears to operate as a constraint on satisfactory conversational exchanges. Grice in [1] blames the inappropriateness of certain kinds of remarks on their violation of constraints such as this. He claims that the goal central to communication - the giving and receiving of information - dictates various co-operative principles as rules of rational behaviour. He cites as a specific maxim that conversationalists should aim to make their contributions as informative as is required for the current purposes of the exchange. Though it is not always unreasonable to violate this maxim, it is clearly reasonable to follow it most of the time, and violations are almost always open to criticism as vague in the non-borderline case sense. The standard of informativeness required in a context depends on the range of alternatives to be discriminated, and this depends on the classification range of the appropriate index.

The same notion of alternative classification ranges throws light on the dependence of borderline case vagueness on context. Whether or not something counts as a borderline case depends on the classification range assumed in the context. If we are watching the enemy advance in the distance and wish to know the colour of the flag they are waving, the alternatives of interest may be just red and white. Orangey-reddish shades will count as red. But in other contexts where exact discrimination of shades is important, and we have a wider range of classifications in mind, the same flag might count as a borderline case of redness.

Or, to take another example, we might accept a classification range consisting just of small and large nails in a context in which the only nails available are all of one or other of two easily distinguishable sizes. (Unless both sorts are either unusually small or large for nails, in which case a wider classification range may come into operation.) The introduction of nails of an intermediate size will produce borderline cases with respect to this range. Inappropriate classification ranges will leave out some items we are able to discriminate in the context. A range which enables observers to classify nails only as small, medium or large will be inappropriate when there is a large range of nails of different sizes available. Where the objects available form a series which appears continuous to a casual observer only a classification range involving a system of precise measurement will do. And where there is a genuine continuum, it seems that there are bound to be borderline cases whatever classification range is adopted. Classification ranges which are inappropriate in this way will inevitably produce borderline cases and so are a source of vagueness. This is not to say they are defective in any sense. Restricted classification ranges may be perfectly acceptable to the participants in a conversation where there is no pressure to decide borderline cases either way. Sorites regresses can be avoided, since these only threaten where observational predicates are employed and, given the limits to the range of discriminations we can actually make, the borderline cases can be distinguished from the correct applications of such predicates.

It is far from clear exactly which classification range is operating in some contexts, even where there appears to be no disagreement on the matter on the part of the participants in the discourse. Thus there will be alternative precisifications of what counts as true enough, alternative reasonable hypotheses about which things are borderline cases, and general unclarity about the standards of precision operating and the level of informativeness required. These uncertainties are obvious sources of Fregean vagueness. Definite boundaries to the range of correct and incorrect applications of a term and to the scope of its borderline cases in a context cannot be laid down if there is doubt about the range of acceptable classifications operating in that context.

I do not know whether this notion of a classification range might be amenable to precise logical treatment: I have only attempted here to make it tolerably clear. But it is certain that no more precise account could supply criteria which would enable us to decide with certainty in every context whether or not the speaker had adopted one precisely described classification range or another. For if this were possible there would be no Fregean vagueness.

Bibliography

VAGUENESS AND RELATED TOPICS

Alston, W. [1] *The Philosophy of Language* Foundations of Philosophy Series Prentice-Hall, Inc. (Englewood Cliffs N.J.) 1964

Anscombe, G.E.M. [1] “The Intentionality of Sensation; A Grammatical Feature” p.158-180 in Butler, R.J. (ed.) *Analytical Philosophy* Second Series. Blackwell (Oxford) 1965

Armstrong, D.M. [1] *A Materialist Theory of the Mind* Routledge and Kegan Paul Ltd. (New York) 1968

Ballmer, T. and Pinkal, M. [1] (eds) *Approaching Vagueness* North-Holland Linguistic Series (Amsterdam, New York, Oxford) 1983

Black, M. [1] "Vagueness" in *The Philosophy of Science* (1937) p.427-455

[2] "Reasoning with Loose Concepts" *Dialogue* Vol II (1963) p.1-12

Bauerle, R. Egli, U. and Von Stechow, A. (eds) [1] *Semantics From Different Points of View* Springer-Verlag (Berlin, Heidelberg, New York) 1979

Campbell, R. [1] "The Sorites Paradox" *Philosophical Studies* 26 (1974) p.175-191

Cargile, J. [1] "The Sorites Paradox" *British Journal for the Philosophy of Science* Vol.20 (1969) p.193-202

Carnap, R. [1] *Meaning and Necessity* Phoenix Books, University of Chicago Press (Chicago and London) 1956

Chandler, H. [1] "Excluded Middle" *Journal of Philosophy* (1967) p.807-814

Chisholm, R.[1] "The Problem of the Speckled Hen" Mind Vol.51 p.368-373

Chomsky, N. [1] *Aspects of the Theory of Syntax* The M.I.T. Press (Cambridge Mass.) 1965

[2] *Rules and Representations* Blackwell (Oxford) 1980

Clark, M. [1] "The Truth about Heaps" *Analysis* 47.4 Oct 1987

Craig, E.J. [1] "The Nature of Sensory Experience" *Synthese* 33 (1976) p.1-23

Cresswell,M. [1] *Logics and Languages* Methuen & Co. (London) 1973
Davidson, D.[1] "Truth and Meaning" *Synthese* 17 (1967) p.304-323
Davies, M.[1] *Meaning, Quantification and Necessity* Routledge and Kegan Paul (London) 1981
Dummett, M.A.E. [1] "Wang's Paradox" *Synthese* 30 (1975) p.325-365
[2] "Common-Sense and Physics" in McDonald, G. (ed.) *Perception and Identity* MacMillan (London) 1979
[3] *Frege* Duckworth (London)
[4] *The Interpretation of Frege's Philosophy* Duckworth (London) 1981
Evans, G.[1] "Can There be Vague Objects?" *Analysis* 38, 1978 p.208
Evans, G. and McDowell, J. (eds.) [1] *Truth and Meaning: Essays in Semantics* Clarendon Press (Oxford) 1976
Field, H. [1] "Quine and the Correspondence Theory" *The Philosophical Review* (1974)
Fine, K.[1] "Vagueness, Truth and Logic" in *Synthese* 30 (1975) p.265-300
Frege, G. [1] "Grundgesetze der Arithmetic" Vol.II section 56 in Geach and Black (eds.) *Selections from the Philosophical Writings of Gotlob Frege* 2nd ed. Blackwell (Oxford) 1970
Freud, S.[1] Vol.IV The Pelican Freud Library Trans. by James Strachey, Penguin Books 1975
Gibson, J.J.[1] *The Senses Considered as Perceptual Systems* Allen and Unwin (London) 1968
Goguen, J.A.[1] "The Logic of Inexact Concepts" *Synthese* 19 (1969) p.325-373
Goodman, N.[1] *Fact, Fiction and Forecast* (Third Edition) Bobbs-Merrill (New York) 1973
[2] *The Structure of Appearance* D.Reidel (Dordecht, Holland) 1977
Gregory, R.L.[1] *Eye and Brain* Weidenfeld and Nicolson (London) 1977
Grice, P.[1]The William James Lectures (unpublished)
[2] "Utterer's Meaning, Sentece Meaning and Word-Meaning" *Foundations of Language* 4 (1968) p.1-18
[3] "Utterer's Meaning and Intentions" *Philosophical Review* 78 (1969) p.147-77
Haack, S.[1] *Deviant Logic* Cambridge University Press (London, New York) 1974

Jackson, F [1] *A Representative Theory of Perception* Cambridge University Press (London, New York) 1977
[2] "Grue" *Journal of Philosophy* Vol. LXXII (1975) p.113-
Jeffrey, R.[1] *Formal Logic; it's Scope and Limits* McGraw-Hill (New York) 1967
Kamp, J.A.W. [1] "Two Theories About Adjectives" in Keenan (ed.) *Formal Semantics of Natural Language* Cambridge University Press (Cambridge) 1975
[2] "The Paradox of the Heap" p.225-277 in Monnich, U. (ed.) *Aspects of Philosophical Logic* D.Reidel (Dordecht, Holland) 1981
Kaplan, A.[1] "Definition and Specification of Meaning" *Journal of Philosophy* Vol.XLIII (1946) p.281-288
Kleene, S.C.[1] *Introduction to Metamathematics* North-Holland (Amsterdam) 1967
Kohl, M.[1] "Bertrand Russell on Vagueness" *Australasian Journal of Philosophy* Vol.147 (1969) p.31-41
King, J.L.[1] "Bivalence and the Sorites Paradox" *American Philosophical Quarterly* Vol.16 (1979) p.17-25
Kripke, S.[1]*Wittgenstein on Rules and Private Language* Blackwell (Oxford) 1982
Krips, H.[1] *The Metaphysics of Quantum Theory* Clarendon Press (New York, Oxford) 1987
Lakatos, I.[1] *The Methodology of Scientific Research Programs* Vol 1. ed Worrall, J. and Currie, G. Cambridge University Press (Cambridge) 1978
Lakoff, G.[1] "Hedges; a Study in Meaning Criteria and the Logic of Fuzzy Concepts" in *Journal of Philsophical Logic* Vol.2 (1973) p.458-508
Lehrer, K. [1] "Coherence, Consensus and Language" *Linguistics and Philsophy* Vol.17, no.1 1984 p.43-55
Lewis, D. [1] *Convention* Harvard University Press (Harvard) 1969
[2] "General Semantics" *Synthese* 22 (1970) p.18-67
[3] "Language and Languages" in Gunderson, K. (ed.) *Minnasota Studies in the Philosophy of Science* Vol.VII Univ. of Minn. Press (Minneapolis) 1975
[4] "Scorekeeping in a Language Game" in Bauerle, Egli and von Stechow (eds.) *Semantics From Different Points of View* p.172-188 1979
[5] "Index, Context and Content" in Kanger and Ohman *Philosophy and Grammar* 1981 p.79-101

Loar, [1] "Two Theories of Meaning" in Evans and McDowell (eds.) *Truth and Meanin* p.138-161

McDowell, J.[1] "Truth Conditions, Bivalence and Verificationism" in Evans and McDowell, *Truth and Meaning* p.42-66

Machina, K.[1] "Vague Predicates" *American Philosophical Quarterly,* Vol.9 (1972) p.225-233

[2] "Truth, Belief and Vagueness" *Journal of Philosophical Logic* 5 (1976) p.47-78

Neisser, U.[1] *Cognition And Reality* W.H.Freeman and Co. (San Francisco) 1979

Noonan, H. [1] "Vague Objects" *Analysis* 1982

Optical Society of America Committee on Colorimetry [1] *The Science of Color* Thomas Y. Crowell (New York) 1956

Peacocke, C.[1] "Are Vague Predicates Incoherent?" in *Synthese* 46 (1981) p.121-141

Pinkal, M.[1] "Towards a Semantics of Precization" in Ballmer and Pinkal (eds) *Approaching Vagueness* North Holland (Amsterdam) 1983

Platts, M. deB. [1] *Ways of Meaning* Routledge and Kegan Paul (London, Henley, Boston) 1979

Putnam, H.[1] "Dreaming and Depth Grammar" p.211-235 in Butler, R.J. (ed) *Analytical Philosophy* First Series Blackwell (Oxford) 1966

[2] "Vagueness and Alternative Logic" *Erkenntnis* 19 (1983) p.297-314

Quine, W.V.O. [1] *Word and Object* M.I.T. Press (Cambridge, Mass.) 1960

[2] *Ontological Relativity and Other Essays* Columbia University Press (New York) 1969

[3] "What Price Bivalence?" *Journal of Philosophy* (1981) p.90-95

Rasmussen,S [1] "Vague Identity" Mind 95 Jan. 1986

Rolf, B.[1] "Sorites" *Synthese* Vol.58 p.219-250

Russell, B.[1] "Vagueness' *Australasian Journal of Philosophy* Vol.1 (1923) p.84-92

[2] *The Analysis of Mind* Allen and Unwin (London) 1929

Sainsbury, M.[1] "Degrees of Belief and Truth" *Philosophical Papers* 15 1986

Sanford [1] "Classical Logic and Inexact Predicates" *Mind* no.83 (1974) 112-113

[2] "Borderline Logic" *American Philosophical Quarterly* Vol.12 (1975) p.29-40

[3] "Competing Semantics of Vagueness; Many Values Versus Supertruth" *Synthese* 33 1976 p.195-210
Scheffler,I.[1] *Beyond the Letter* Routledge and Kegan Paul (London, Boston, Henley) 1979
Schiffer,S [1] *Meaning* Oxford University Press (London) 1972
Schwartz,S.[1] "Intuitionism and the Sorites" *Analysis* 47.4 1987
Suppe, F.[1] *The Structure of Scientific Theories* University of Illinois Press (Urbana) 1977
Tarski, A.[1] *Logic, Semantics and Metamathematics; Papers from 1921-1938"* trans. by Woodger, J.H. Clarendon Press (Oxford) 1956
Taylor, B.[1] "States of Affairs" in Evans and McDowell (eds) *Truth and Meaning* p.263-284
Thomason, R.[1] "Identity and Vagueness" *Philosophical Studies* 1982
Thorpe, D.[1] "The Sorites Paradox" *Synthese* 61 (1984)
Travis, C.[1] "Vagueness, Observation and the Sorites" *Mind* 94 1985
Unger, P. [1] "There are No Ordinary Things" *Synthese* 41 (1979) p.117-154
[2] "I Do Not Exist" in McDonald, G. *Perception and Identity* MacMillan (London) 1979
Waismann, F. [1] "Verifiability" *Proceedings of the Aristotelean Society,* Supp. Vol.19 (1954), pp.119-50
Wheeler, S.[1] "Reference and Vagueness' *Synthese* 30 (1975) p.367-379
[2] "On That Which Is Not" *Synthese* 41 (1979) p.155-173
White [1] "Slippery Slope Arguments" *Metaphilosophy* 1985
Wittgenstein, L. [1] *Philosophical Investigations* trans. by Anscombe, G.E.M. Blackwell (Oxford) 1963
Wright, C. [1] "On the Coherence of Vague Predicates" *Synthese* 30 (1975) p.325-365
[2] "Rule-Following Objectivity and the Theory of Meaning" in Holzmann and Leich (eds) *Wittgenstein; To Follow a Rule* Routledge and Kegan Paul (London, Boston, Henley)
[3] "Strict Finitism" *Synthese* 51 (1982) p.203-282
Zadeh, L.[1] "Fuzzy Logic and Approximate Reasoning" *Synthese* (1975) p.407-495

Index

REASON AND ARGUMENT

Publications:

1. J. Norman and R. Sylvan (eds.): *Directions in Relevant Logic*. In Memory of Alan Ross Anderson. 1989 ISBN 0-7923-0386-5
2. J.T.J. Srzednicki (ed.): *Initiatives in Logic*. 1987 ISBN 90-247-3600-5
3. E. Żarnecka-Biały (ed.): *Logic Counts*. 1990 ISBN 0-7923-0942-1
4. L. Burns: *Vagueness*. 1991 ISBN 0-7923-1489-1

KLUWER ACADEMIC PUBLISHERS – DORDRECHT / BOSTON/ LONDON